THE KEYS TO CONFLICT RESOLUTION

PROVEN METHODS OF
SETTLING DISPUTES VOLUNTARILY

THE KEYS TO

Conflict Resolution

PROVEN METHODS OF
SETTLING DISPUTES VOLUNTARILY

BY *Theodore W. Kheel*

FOUR WALLS EIGHT WINDOWS
NEW YORK · LONDON

Published in the United States by:
Four Walls Eight Windows
39 West 14th Street, room 503
New York, N.Y., 10011

U.K. offices:
Four Walls Eight Windows/Turnaround
Unit 3, Olympia Trading Estate
Coburg Road, Wood Green
London N22 6TZ, England

Visit our website at http://www.fourwallseightwindows.com

First printing April 1999.

Library of Congress Cataloging-in-Publication Data:
Kheel, Theodore W.
The Keys to Conflict Resolution: Proven Methods of Settling Disputes Voluntarily / by Theodore W. Kheel
p.   cm.
ISBN 1-56858-134-3
1. Dispute resolution (Law)—United States. 2. Compromise (Law)—United States. 3. Arbitration and award—United States. 4. Mediation—United States. 5. Negotiation—United States. I. Title.
KF9084.K48   1999
347.73'9–dc21   98-55581
                                              CIP

10 9 8 7 6 5 4 3 2 1

Designed by Abe Lerner

Typeset by Precision Typographers

Printed in the United States

"They did not fully understand the technique.
In a very short time they nearly wrecked the planet."

Words appearing in a 1972 work of art
by Robert Rauschenberg

CONTENTS

PREFACE

Alternative Dispute Resolution and the
Voluntary Techniques of Conflict Resolution

Conflicts are proliferating throughout the world. They are threatening to overwhelm us. Fortunately, a counterforce is gaining popularity. It goes by the name of Alternative Dispute Resolution, but is more frequently called ADR, its acronym.

ADR came into prominence as a result of company and individual dissatisfaction over the increasing costs and delays of lawsuits.

In 1997 and again in 1998, *Forbes* magazine promoted a Superconference on ADR as a way industry could save millions in legal expenses. *Forbes* went so far as to say that ADR is a "revolutionary trend" that is spreading throughout the world.

But ADR is far more than a way of saving time and money on litigation. It is a call for self-reliance, a way of living in harmony with our neighbors, an endorsement of voluntarism.

As Pogo famously said, "We have met the enemy and he is us."* Nothing stands between us and disaster except ourselves. This principle applies to nuclear war as it does to resolving—peacefully, voluntarily, without guns or lawyers—a dispute between neighbors in suburbia over how early it's permissible for a lawnmower to break the morning silence.

Anyone with a claim against another person can start a lawsuit. All you have to do is serve your opponent with a summons and complaint. Of course you have to have what the lawyers call a cause of action to get anywhere in the courts. But you don't need your opponent's consent to resolve the dispute in the courts.

There are, and always have been, three practical alternatives to litigation: negotiation, mediation and arbitration. There is, however, a catch. Neither mediation nor arbitration can be invoked unless both sides first negotiate an agreement to use either of those techniques.

Negotiation is not only an essential prelude to mediation and arbitration. It underlies and informs our entire system of conflict resolution. Negotiation began when Adam and Eve arrived on the planet.

---

*Unlike Pogo, I would say "he or she" is us. But I hereafter use the masculine without repeated mention of the feminine solely to economize on words.

Mediation followed shortly thereafter, when the serpent charmed Eve into eating an apple from the Tree of Knowledge.

Arbitration is a latter-day development founded on negotiation and mediation.

Any and all disputes, including disputes over invoking mediation and arbitration, can be resolved through negotiation. Negotiation is actually the main alternative to litigation; indeed, far more disputes are settled through negotiation than are decided by courts. Mediation and arbitration are useful adjuncts of negotiation. Together, the three are what I call the voluntary techniques of conflict resolution.

In addition to saving time and money, the voluntary techniques can resolve disputes the courts can't handle. The courts can only resolve "rights" disputes, or disputes over whether a law or contract has been violated. They cannot resolve "interest" disputes, or disputes over claims that do not state what the lawyers call a cause of action.

No court, for example, can tell a seller to take less or a buyer to pay more. Nor can a court rule on the terms and provisions to be included in a new or renegotiated contract. Only the parties themselves can settle such disputes.

Interest disputes far outnumber the rights disputes that the courts can handle. Together with rights disputes, they can be resolved through the voluntary techniques. The ability of the disputants to agree with each other on using voluntary techniques is the only limit on their outreach. They are the "do it together" techniques of conflict resolution. They challenge all of us to learn to get along with each other.

While ADR's voluntary alternatives can be used by just about anyone, simply favoring them is not, by itself, enough. To be effective, they require skills that must be wisely deployed. If we fail to learn how to take advantage of ADR's important message, we potentially face not only divine wrath but chaos right here on earth.

INTRODUCTION

By William L. Lurie*

Sam and Kate Kheel disagreed what to name their first son. Sam, who had run unsuccessfully for Congress in 1912 on Theodore Roosevelt's Bull Moose ticket, favored "Theodore" even though Roosevelt had lost the presidency to Woodrow Wilson. Kate thought they should name him "Woodrow" for the winner. They resolved the dispute by agreeing on Theodore Woodrow Kheel.

Kheel does not claim that he inherited his interest in conflict resolution from his parents. He says he came to it by chance. Kheel graduated from Cornell University Law School in 1937. The country was then in the midst of a recession, following a mild recovery from the depression that began with the stock market crash of 1929. Like many others, Kheel had difficulty finding a job. Although he had no prior experience in labor-management relations, he finally landed one on the legal staff of the National Labor Relations Board at a yearly salary of $2,000.

On his first day on the job, Kheel had no sooner sat down when the President of the Lawyer's Division of the National Labor Relations Board Union entered his office and asked Kheel when he got out of law school and how much he was being paid. Upon being told, he advised Kheel that under the union's contract with the Board he was entitled to $2,600 a year and urged him to file a grievance. When a look of apprehension appeared on Kheel's face, he quickly added, "If you don't, the union will." Kheel filed the grievance and his salary was quickly raised to $2,600.

When the Japanese bombed Pearl Harbor and the United States entered the war, Kheel moved to the National War Labor Board, a tripartite agency composed of an equal number of public, labor and management representatives. The board had been created by President Franklin D. Roosevelt to maintain labor peace during the war. Kheel quickly rose in the ranks and in due course became the Board's executive director. During his years with the board, Kheel spent much of

---

*Wiliam L. Lurie was formerly president of the Business Roundtable.

Kheel (center), as executive director of the National War Labor Board, attending a 1943 meeting at the Ford Motor Company's Willow Run Plant in Michigan with other WLB officers and associates on the critical impact of labor disputes on the war effort.

his time resolving labor disputes that might interfere with the war effort.

When the war ended, Kheel returned to New York and became active as an assistant to Mayor William O'Dwyer in mediating a rash of post-war labor disputes. Included among the conflicts he handled were several major disputes arising out of the introduction of technologies that displaced workers. These technologies were generally grouped under the name automation. In seeking solutions, Kheel recognized that the labor-management relationship combines two conflicting elements. As participants in an on-going relationship, both sides have a stake in the success of the enterprise. But they are and will always be in conflict over the division of the rewards.

The companies pointed to the increased efficiency and cost reductions that automation could bring. The unions complained about the loss of jobs. In a speech that attracted wide attention, George Meany, then president of the AFL-CIO, called automation a curse, sounding much like the Luddites of the 19th century who smashed textile machines that were displacing them. The battle was intense.

In discussions with leaders of labor and management, Kheel pointed out that automation could not and should not be stopped. Further, he said it was essential for both sides to address the concerns of the workers not only as a matter of fairness but also because it made good business sense.

The discussions led Kheel, with others from labor and management, to form the American Foundation on Automation and Employment and for Kheel to serve as its executive director. Their aim was to assist in advancing automation by addressing the employment problems it was creating. The foundation played a leading role in identifying the respective concerns of labor and management, a first step towards successful conflict resolution. With Kheel participating as the board's executive director, the foundation also helped in devising solutions to conflicts in specific situations.

As he became more deeply involved in labor management relations, Kheel began to see conflict resolution as an indispensable part of industrial life. He also recognized that controlled conflict could produce creative solutions.

As an industrial peacemaker, Ted Kheel has brought inventiveness and daring to the solution of countless seemingly intractable disputes in both the public and private sectors at local and national levels. *Business Week* called Kheel the "Master Locksmith of Deadlock

1947: Mayor William O'Dwyer swearing in Kheel (center)
as New York City's Director of Labor Relations, and
Joseph O'Grady as Deputy Director, as Kheel's mother,
Kate Kheel, and predecessor director, Edward Maguire,
look on.

Bargaining." He has been a member of numerous fact-finding boards appointed by presidents, governors and mayors and has participated in the resolution of more than 30,000 labor grievances.

Kheel is a New York original. Born in that city in 1914, he was a partner of Battle Fowler from 1949 to 1983 and has since been of counsel to the law firm. Kheel is a businessman as well as a lawyer and mediator and has served on the board of directors of several prominent companies.

A former president of the National Urban League (which seeks to ease racial tensions), he was also the principal founder of several foundations that address various types of conflicts. They include, among others, the Institute of Mediation and Conflict Resolution, a not-for-profit group prominently involved in the settlement of community dis-

Kheel, serving as Director of New York City's Division of Labor Relations, speaking for Mayor O'Dwyer in Chicago, Illinois in 1948 at the convention of the Transport Workers Union.

putes, the Institute of Collective Bargaining and Group Relations, now affiliated with Cornell University's School of Industrial and Labor Relations, the Foundation on Prevention and Early Resolution of Conflict, the Labor-Management Distance Learning Foundation, and the Earth Pledge Foundation, which seeks to bridge the conflict between environmental development and economic growth. For over twenty-five years Kheel has represented the internationally renowned artist Robert Rauschenberg, whose 1972 work of art contains words Kheel has adopted as a theme of his book.

Kheel's purpose in writing this book is to help people understand and make better use of Alternative Dispute Resolution and the voluntary techniques of conflict resolution. Based on his more than 50 years of practical experience, the book is sure to fulfill his purpose.

ACKNOWLEDGEMENTS

I am indebted to my wife, Ann S. Kheel, and the following friends and experts, whose names I am listing in alphabetical order, for the invaluable advice, assistance and guidance they gave me in the composition of this book. I am also indebted to the many persons who partook in the various negotiations I have included in the book. They are too numerous to mention. Besides, they were not aware at the time that I was learning from them about the voluntary techniques of conflict resolution.

- William L. Lurie, former President of the Business Roundtable
- Charles Markham, Attorney and former Mayor of Durham, North Carolina
- David E. Pitt, Chief Writer, United Nations Children's Fund (UNICEF)
- Richard Strassberg, Director, Kheel Center for Labor-Management Documentation and Archives at Cornell University and Meg Joseph of the same organization
- Sheldon Zalaznick, former Managing Editor of *Forbes* Magazine

I am also indebted to my colleagues at Battle Fowler for the pleasures I derived from my many years with the law firm and to Valerie Anderson and Elizabeth Surcouf for their expert assistance in preparing the manuscript for publication.

THE KEYS TO CONFLICT RESOLUTION

PROVEN METHODS OF
SETTLING DISPUTES VOLUNTARILY

CHAPTER ONE

STRENGTHS AND LIMITATIONS
OF THE VOLUNTARY TECHNIQUES

WE have been encouraged to prevent and resolve disputes almost since the beginning of time. The Bible tells us to "love thy neighbor as thyself," a prime technique of conflict resolution.

The Bible also has good words for those who try to prevent or resolve disputes. "Blessed are the peacemakers," it says, "for they shall be called the children of God." Shakespeare expressed a similar sentiment. Confining himself to this planet, he simply said, "Blessed are the peacemakers on earth."

Most of the conflicts I discuss in this book are between identifiable individuals or groups possessing either the power to reach binding agreements or the authority to recommend resolution to principals who have the power to reach final agreement.

The voluntary techniques of conflict resolution function in much the same manner in all types of conflicts, domestic or international, even including those that society condemns—extortion, blackmail or kidnapping, for example. While exercising care to avoid being caught, the culprits invariably negotiate with their victims on what they want from them.

The disputants, the issues in dispute and the circumstances are variables that distinguish one conflict from another. They affect, but do not alter, the mechanics of the voluntary techniques of conflict resolution.

Once the variables are mastered, the techniques can be applied with equal effectiveness in any and all types of disputes.

While negotiators' skills (or lack of them) and their relative bargaining strength generally outweigh personal influences, such traits as pride, conceit, ambition and jealousy can frequently affect the outcome. Personal likes and dislikes can also be a factor.

A big ego, for example, may sometimes be helpful. But it can also get in the way. I've seen many a disputant snatch defeat from the jaws of victory as his personal ambitions overwhelmed his better judgment.

"The gentle art of losing face," a seasoned negotiator once told me, "may some day save the human race."

Being True to the Role You Are Playing

There are not only many variables within each of the recognized techniques of conflict resolution; there are also varying roles the disputants and third party neutrals play.

A negotiator's aim is to get the best deal for his side.

A mediator seeks to bring the negotiators together.

An arbitrator decides how the dispute should be resolved.

Each role has its own requirements. A participant in conflict resolution should be clear on the role he is playing and remain faithful to it during the course of the dispute. A departure can be damaging.

At the invitation of Mayor Robert F. Wagner, I became the mediator in the 1962/63 conflict between the major newspapers of New York City and Local Six of the International Typographical Union, one of ten unions representing employees of the newspapers. Amory H. Bradford, vice president and general manager of the *New York Times,* was the chief negotiator for the Publishers Association, which at the time represented ten New York City newspapers. Bertram Powers, president of the union, was the union's chief spokesman.

During the months before I became involved, Bradford dominated the procedural aspects of the negotiations: when and where the meetings should be held, whether they should be joint or separate, the order in which the issues should be considered, when the negotiations should be recessed and then reconvened etc. At the outset of my involvement, I clashed frequently with Bradford on these procedural matters. It is far better for the mediator, rather than one of the negotiators, to be in charge of these procedural matters. He can resolve them without influencing the outcome of the substantive issues on which the negotiators must retain the right to make the final decision.

After several weeks of bickering with Bradford, I concluded that I could not be effective as mediator in face of his continued insistence on determining how the mediation should be conducted. In the circumstances, I decided and announced that I was resigning. Since each side is entitled to chose whomever they want to represent them, I did not make Bradford's removal a condition of my continued participation.

Orvil E. Dryfoos, then publisher of the *New York Times,* sought me out and pleaded with me not to resign. He said that he was convinced that Powers was out to destroy the *Times.* While I did not believe that was Powers's goal, I agreed to stay on. Without my asking, Dryfoos withdrew Bradford from the negotiations. Jack Flynn of the *New York Daily News* and Walter Thayer of the *New York Herald Tribune* took over in behalf of the Publishers Association. Their better understanding of the rules of the game helped produce an agreement that both sides ultimately ratified.

The Importance of Defining the Issues and Asssessing the Facts

If there is one major lesson I have learned about the resolution of conflicts, it is the importance of defining the issues in dispute at the earliest possible date. Surprisingly, even the most sophisticated negotiators sometimes fail to address this aspect of conflict resolution. In so doing, they frequently waste time and effort on matters that may not be in controversy and irritate each other by making claims that obscure their basic differences.

It is also important to get the facts offered in support of the claims properly identified and assessed for accuracy and relevance. As William H. Davis, a distinguished patent lawyer who served as Chairman of the National War Labor Board, often observed, "You can't argue about a fact, you can only be ignorant of it." But disputants nevertheless frequently argue about the facts. Like politicians, they will "spin" the facts to favor their side. Even so, the exercise in getting the facts straight can, by itself, help immeasurably in bringing a dispute to a successful conclusion.

Another point of importance—focusing on procedure before substance—also deserves mention. The value of addressing procedure first was dramatically confirmed by the unanimous vote of a sharply divided United States Senate on how President Clinton's impeachment should be conducted. Issues of procedure rarely engender the intense feelings substantive issues incite. Besides, agreement on procedure generally gets the negotiations off on a positive note.

Simple as the points I am making may sound, they are essential in reaching settlements or, at the least, in narrowing the differences between the disputants.

Framing the Issues Precisely

The way an issue is framed can dictate the answer; even seemingly innocuous phrasing can make a difference. As the *New York Times* reported, a small change in the wording of a question by the Gallup Organization led to a significant overstatement of the drop in President Clinton's personal favorability rating after his August 17, 1998 speech confessing that he had misled the public in denying that he had an affair with Monica Lewinsky.

In a poll taken a week before his speech, the wording was, "Now I'd like to get your opinion about some people in the news. As I read the name, please say if you have a favorable or unfavorable opinion of this person." That traditional wording resulted in public impressions of Mr. Clinton that were 60% favorable and 38% unfavorable.

In a survey conducted immediately after his speech, Gallup asked respondents, "Now thinking about Bill Clinton as a person, do you have a favorable or unfavorable opinion of him?" The responses from the public were 40% favorable and 48% unfavorable, a huge shift in opinion.

In another poll conducted on the day after his speech. Gallup used the traditional wording and measured 55% with favorable views of Mr. Clinton and 42% unfavorable, a far less dramatic shift.

*   *   *

When pollsters ask respondents if they favor or oppose equal opportunity, most will say they are in favor of it. If they are asked about affirmative action, many will likely respond in the negative. But affirmative action is simply the nametag of programs to advance equal opportunity. How opportunities can be made equal and what actions are appropriate to make them equal calls for careful definition of the terms.

The meaning that people attach to specific words related to equal opportunity and affirmative action frequently arouse emotional responses. The word "quota" is one. Quotas can help correct past denials but they tend to be viewed as a denial of equal opportunity. On the other hand, training to help applicants qualify will generally draw support.

Does equal opportunity mean that the applicant best able to perform the job must always be selected? If so, how are the respective skills of the applicants to be measured? Should applicants for admission to a college or university, for example, be judged solely on the basis of their

ACT and SAT scorecards? Should an applicant's extra-curricular attainments be considered? Can the advantages to the college or university and the other students of a racially balanced student body or work force in our pluralistic society be taken into account? Defining what is meant by the terms is an indispensable prerequisite to fair solutions.

* * *

Opponents on the issue of abortion use the catch phrases "pro choice" and "pro life" to gain adherents to their respective positions. As phrases, it is difficult to be against either of them. Obscured behind the phrases is the central question of whether life begins at the moment of conception, as some believe, or when the fetus becomes viable, as others contend.

The Supreme Court drew a line of distinction between the first and succeeding trimesters of pregnancy and concluded that abortion should not be barred during the first trimester. Those who believe that life begins at conception remain opposed to the decision. Hardly anyone would favor abortion to end a pregnancy in the ninth month. A majority appears to have no problem with a morning-after approach. A narrower issue in the continuing debate is where and how the line should be drawn after the first trimester.

* * *

I recently spoke at a forum on drug control, pointing out that the issue of whether drugs should be legalized was misleading since it seemed to suggest that if legalized, hard drugs could become as available as any over-the-counter drug. But a doctor's prescription is necessary before anyone can buy most sleeping pills and antibiotics. Surely the advocates of legalizing drugs would not make cocaine and heroin more readily available than those far milder drugs. The requirement of a doctor's prescription is a form of drug regulation. The sharper question is how hard drugs should be regulated, not whether they should be legalized.

* * *

The identification of areas of common interest can frequently assist in the resolution of conflicts in on-going group relationships. The labor-management relationship provides a good example. In the parlance of game theory, it is sometimes described as a relationship that combines conflict with cooperation. It is in labor's interest for the company to succeed, since the better a company does, the more there is for the employees to seek. Union leaders understand this mutuality of interest and may even go so far as to oppose environmental restrictions that might hurt a company's business. Others will advocate tariffs that limit foreign competition. I have also seen unions come to the aid of management in take-over battles. But they will quarrel intensely over their share of the fruits of success.

At the insistence of Morton Bahr, the President of the Communications Workers of America, joined later by the International Brotherhood of Electrical Workers, AT&T agreed in collective bargaining to a joint educational program they call the Alliance for Employee Growth and Development. Lucent Technologies became a party to the Alliance after it was spun off from AT&T. Some of the so-called Baby Bells have adopted similar programs as have companies in the steel, auto, aerospace and several other industries.

The unions see the programs as safety nets enabling employees to acquire skills they can market in the event of downsizing. Management endorses the programs because it makes better trained employees available. By defining their mutual interests, labor and management can create an atmosphere of cooperation that can help them resolve their unavoidable conflicts over the mandatory subjects of bargaining, wages, hours and working conditions.

Defining the Terms of Conflict Resolution

The terms that describe the techniques of conflict resolution are sometimes misunderstood, even at the highest levels.

I was watching a basketball game on TV the night of April 9, 1964, when an announcer interrupted to say that President Lyndon B. Johnson had secured a 15-day postponement of a strike that threatened to shut down the nation's 523 railroads. The announcer also reported that "new negotiators" would be entering the dispute.

I was relieved to hear that the President had managed to avert the threatened strike. Historians now say that this was Johnson's first major crisis after becoming President following Kennedy's assassination on November 22, 1963. But as a professional in the business of conflict resolution, I was puzzled about the introduction of new *negotiators*. Each side in a dispute invariably names its own negotiators. It would be unusual for either side to agree in a mediation session to change the negotiators who were representing them.

As I was reflecting on what Johnson meant, the telephone rang and

Kheel, as president of the National Urban League in the 1960s, conferring on civil rights with then-Vice President Lyndon B. Johnson.

my wife answered. "It's for you," she called, and I reached for the phone. "Mr. Kheel?" an operator inquired. When I said "yes," he quickly announced, "the President of the United States."

"Ted," the President said (I had met with him several times on conflict resolution in race relations when he was vice-president), "we need new negotiators down here. Can you be at the White House first thing tomorrow morning?" I not only agreed but left almost immediately to catch the last shuttle to Washington. I realized, of course, that I was being asked to be a mediator in the railroad dispute, not a negotiator for one side or the other. The President of the United States, like many others, had confused the terms.

The confusion was harmless. I knew what the President meant and he knew that I would be serving as a mediator. At the risk of oversimplification, I am including the following definitions of the principal terms of conflict resolution.

I use the words *conflict* and *dispute* interchangeably to mean any difference between two or more "persons" growing out of "some matter" that one person wants from another. The person can be an individual or a group entity such as a corporation, union, government agency and even a nation itself. The matter can be anything under the sun.

Pick up this morning's newspaper and scan the front page: you will surely find at least one story on a political, business, labor, environmental, communal, social or sports conflict over some matter that one or more persons, as defined, wants from another person or persons.

The term "resolution" is easy to define. It means bringing the conflict or dispute to an end. But there are many ways in which the dispute can be resolved. Disputes can be abandoned by one side or the other or they can be ended by force. My focus is on the resolution of disputes through the voluntary techniques of negotiation, mediation and arbitration.

Mediation is simply an adjunct to negotiation. The mediator's job is to help the disputants reach agreement. The structure of mediation is discussed in Chapter Four.

The term arbitration is also easy to define. It is the resolution of a conflict by the decision of a third party appointed pursuant to an agreement between the disputants. Arbitration is discussed in Chapter Six.

We are all myopic and necessarily see things from our own point of view. And we rarely reflect on the other side's perspective. To see ourselves as others see us is a talent the Scottish poet Robert Burns admired, as he wrote in his poem "To a Louse."* It is a skill every negotiator should seek to possess if he doesn't instinctively reflect on how his opponent sees him.

There is an opposite gift negotiators should also possess: the ability to see others as they see themselves. By so doing, they can better devise strategies that will be persuasive in influencing their opponent to agree to give them what they want. Understanding these principles is fundamental. Sometimes even the most experienced negotiators fall short on both counts.

In a recent negotiation over the clean-up of a polluted site on the Hudson River involving ARCO, the giant oil company, I was representing a small not-for-profit organization known as the Earth Pledge Foundation, which I helped found in 1991 to advance the principles of

---

*"Oh wad some power the giftie gie us/To see oursels as ithers see us!"

sustainable development, i.e., development that promotes economic growth without damaging the environment. The site involved had been contaminated with hazardous wastes over the course of more than a hundred years. ARCO was legally liable to clean up the site since it had bought and absorbed Anaconda Copper and Wire, the company originally responsible for the contamination.

As a not-for-profit foundation committed to sustainable development, we hoped to prove that in a cooperative effort with ARCO and the relevant government agencies and community organizations, we could reclaim a polluted site and restore it to sound economic use. We thought we were in agreement on the general principles of our joint effort as we set about to reduce them to writing. ARCO undertook to prepare the first drafts of the relevant documents and they retained a prominent law firm for that purpose.

It became clear upon reading the drafts that ARCO and Earth Pledge had totally different ideas on how we could work together. ARCO's lawyer, who had not taken part in the negotiations and did not consult us before preparing the drafts, saw the agreement solely from ARCO's point of view. From my viewpoint the drafts failed to take into account the reasons we had expressed during our negotiations for wanting to work with ARCO on remediation as well as development.

But the drafts served a useful purpose. They brought into focus the fundamental differences between us that we had not considered when we simply agreed that it would be advantageous for us to work together.

Our agreement on general principles was not nearly enough. Whether we could have reached a definitive agreement is problematical. We never did. But we would have had a better chance and, at the least, we could have saved time and energy if we had tried at an earlier date to define the issues in light of our respective purposes.

The Alternatives of Alternative Dispute Resolution

A number of voluntary techniques of conflict resolution in addition to mediation and arbitration are sometimes cited as alternatives to litigation. Actually, they are simply variants of mediation and arbitration that can be categorized by ascertaining who has the power to make the final decision of resolution.

If the disputants themselves retain the right to make the final decision, the alternative is a form of mediation; if a third party makes the final decision, it is a form of arbitration. Here are some examples of these variants and how they can be identified as a form of mediation or arbitration:

• **Advisory Arbitration** is a form of mediation conducted as an arbitration with the disputants retaining the right to reject the advisory arbitrator's award. In effect, the "decision" of the "advisory arbitrator" is a recommendation dressed in the clothing of a final and binding award. But the "award" does not end the dispute unless both parties accept the recommendations. In composing his decision, the advisory arbitrator's overriding concern should be the same as a mediator's: to get the parties to agree with each other. In pursuance of that objective, he is well advised to focus on what both sides are likely to accept as well as the merits of the dispute.

• **Mini-trial** is a hearing conducted as if it were a lawsuit. But it must be viewed as a form of mediation since the "decision" of the judge or judges in a mini-trial is not binding. It is merely a recommendation with the disputants themselves retaining the right to reject the decision and to make the final decision of agreement or disagreement.

• **Fact-finding** can be extremely useful if the facts are in dispute and fact-finders are also frequently called upon to make recommendations. In a railroad or airline dispute that threatens to create a national emergency, the President can by law appoint a fact-finding board that is also called upon to make recommendations to resolve the dispute. In many of such disputes, the facts are not seriously in dispute. You might even say they have never been lost. In such cases, the recommendations are generally the most significant part of the board's report. But the report is nonetheless a form of mediation since the fact-finders' recommendations are not final or binding. They have served their main purpose only if both sides accept the recommendations.

• **Med-Arb**, as its name implies, encourages the neutral party to mediate at first but, if mediation is unsuccessful, to make a binding award on unresolved issues. It becomes third party decision-making in the second stage and is definitely a form of arbitration.

• **Tripartite Boards of Arbitration** usually consist of one arbitrator named by each party and a third arbitrator picked jointly by the two party-appointed arbitrators or named by an impartial service provider such as the American Arbitration Association.

While it is not unexpected for the appointed arbitrators to favor the party that appointed them, they are arbitrators and their vote has the same force as the vote of the neutral arbitrator. Nor is the party-appointed arbitrator prohibited from consulting the party that appointed him during the course of the board's deliberations.

In consequence, at least one of the party-appointed arbitrators must join the neutral to make a final and binding award. Three separate decisions would be the equivalent of a tie and would be of no force or effect.

As a practical matter, the neutral arbitrator will frequently try to secure a unanimous award. If unsuccessful, he will then try to persuade one of the appointed arbitrators to join him in making a majority decision. These considerations often lead to a negotiation within the board that resembles the original negotiation of the parties.

Even though the party-appointed arbitrators are, in a sense, stand-ins for the disputants, they are usually more objective and less emotional than the disputants themselves. As a result, the arbitrators often produce a solution satisfactory to both sides.

Arbitration by boards of party-appointed arbitrators in addition to a neutral arbitrator works best in interest disputes where compromise is not unexpected. They are less useful in disputes over the meaning and application of law or contracts. In such disputes, they rarely add anything more to the arbitration than cost and time.

• **Final Offer Selection** is a form of arbitration. As the name implies, it places a limitation on the authority of the arbitrator who must accept the final offer of one side or the other. He cannot arrive at a compromise decision. This approach has been incorporated in the collective bargaining agreements in professional baseball.

• **Judicial Mediation** occurs when judges with the ultimate right and power to decide the dispute seek to mediate before making a final decision.

Many authorities question whether it is wise for judges to mix mediation with final decision making. Nor are the disputants likely to be as frank with the judge. Such authorities recommend instead that judges, sensing that the dispute might be settled, should refer the dispute to a mediator.

Many courts now have mediation procedures available for such contingencies. Wisely, they make it clear that, in the event the dispute is not settled, nothing said during mediation can be used in court.

- **Legislative Action** can also be a method of conflict resolution. But the disputants themselves can neither initiate nor control the action. They can, of course, spark legislative interest and they also can speak up firmly in lobbying the legislature to act in their favor. But they have no voice in the final decision.

CHAPTER TWO

THE STRUCTURE OF NEGOTIATION: THE PRIMARY TECHNIQUE OF CONFLICT RESOLUTION

THE dictionary defines negotiation, the main technique of conflict resolution, by saying that it is the action or process of negotiating and that to negotiate is to confer with another so as to arrive at a settlement of some matter.

All of us are constantly engaged in negotiation during our waking hours. A negotiation is dynamic. It can even be taking place as we sleep.

Negotiation goes under many names. As Shakespeare said, "What's in a name? That which we call a rose by any other name would smell as sweet." In foreign affairs, the dictionary tells us, diplomacy is the "art and practice of conducting *negotiations* between nations."

In the relations of labor and management, negotiation is known as collective bargaining. It is defined in the National Labor Relations Act as "the mutual obligation of the employer and the representative of the employees to meet at reasonable times and confer in good faith with respect to wages, hours and other terms and conditions of employment." In politics, special interest groups engage in lobbying. Not-for-profit organizations appeal for contributions. Beggars plead for alms.

Whether they know it or not, they are all engaged in negotiation.

Negotiation: A Game of Strategy

In his book "The Strategy of Conflict," Professor Thomas C. Schelling of Harvard University uses the term "strategy" from games theory to indicate a game in which the best course of action for each player depends on what the other player or players do. According to Schelling, such a game is intended to focus on the interdependence of the adversaries' decisions and on their expectations about each other's behavior as distinguished from games of chance which turn on pure luck and games of skill that depend primarily on the talents of the players.

The test of whether the game is one of skill, chance or strategy depends on the predominant characteristic of the game.

A game of tennis, for example, is definitely a game of skill, as any amateur quickly discovers if he gets on the court with a pro. Roulette is a game of chance and weight lifting a game of pure skill.

Negotiation is predominantly a game of strategy even though it requires skill and there can be elements of chance that affect the outcome. The moves each side makes towards reaching an agreement on terms that satisfy their respective interests necessarily turn on the moves the other side makes.

Negotiation: A Skill Enhanced Through Training and Practice

Every one of us spends more time during our waking hours negotiating with each other than we spend in any other social activity. We may not always be aware that we are engaged in negotiation. We rarely think of ourselves as negotiating when we differ with our spouse over what movie to see. But even such simple debates come within the definition of negotiation I found in a dictionary: discussions aimed at agreement.

No one has to be trained or licensed to negotiate. Negotiation comes naturally. A baby is negotiating when he cries for milk. Doing it well is an art, not a science. While some people are born negotiators, the skills of negotiation can be enhanced and sharpened through training and practice.

It is sometimes said that negotiation should be conducted on a level playing field. That ideal would call for both sides to possess relatively equal bargaining strength, to be equally sophisticated in bargaining strategies and to enjoy the same good or bad fortune in the negotiations.

But in real life, of course, the playing field is never completely level. The main difference is usually the relative bargaining strength and skills of the respective negotiators.

Changing the Status Quo

Negotiation is about changing the status quo. If both parties are satisfied with the way things are, there is nothing for them to negotiate about. A negotiable issue over a change in the status quo may come into play if, for example, a seller wants a price increase, a union seeks a raise, a landlord a rent hike, a nation the territory of another nation.

Sometimes, both sides want to change the status quo. On other occasions, the demands of the moving party may provoke an opponent into advancing counter proposals. On occasion counter proposals are advanced for strategic reasons.

The Burden of Going Forward

The party seeking a change in the status quo has the burden of going forward with his proposals. If they are rejected, the party in control remains in possession of the status quo. It is then up to the party seeking a change to decide whether to accept the status quo and abandon the negotiations or to take steps that shift the burden of responding to the other side.

In negotiating new or successor collective bargaining agreements, labor and management frequently engage in such exchanges. In times past, their negotiations most often began with a union's demand for a wage increase. If in the end, the employer rejected the increase, the union's traditional response was to strike. But a strike is costly and unions now think twice before calling one.

In many cases in recent times, employers have become the moving party on changes in the status quo. If the employer proposes a wage decrease or other reduction in employment terms or conditions and the union refuses to accept the cut, the employer can legally lock out the employees if he has first bargained in good faith to an impasse.

While a lockout is generally seen as the opposite to a strike, employers have a better option. They can unilaterally impose the changes in the status quo they have proposed provided, again, that they have bargained in good faith to an impasse before making the changes. The monkey is then on the union's back. The union can either accept the change the employer has imposed or strike.

For strategic reasons, the owners and players in baseball and basketball pursued opposite courses in bargaining on the skyrocketing player salaries in professional sports. In baseball the players struck for 234 days over the owners' proposal of a cap on the salaries of all players. In basketball, the owners locked the players out in a dispute over changes in the salary cap they had previously negotiated. The final settlement included an unprecedented cap on individual salaries based on years of service. As discussed in Chapter Nine, the turmoil in professional sports is an outgrowth of the two tier system of bargaining: individual bargaining on salaries and collective bargaining on everything else.

The Life Cycle of a Negotiation

As in many contests, the life cycle of a negotiation usually consists of three stages. They may occur in a brief span or over a long period of time. In typical transactions, the parties exchange demands in stage one, discuss them in stage two and reach conclusions in stage three.

In complex disputes, the parties will enlarge on their goals in the first stage, indicating not only what they want or will give but why. For the most part, the issues at this stage are discussed in general terms with questions posed for clarification. But at all stages, the parties are looking for telltale signs of what their opponent is really seeking to get out of the negotiations. As I have previously noted, the parties should clearly identify the issue or issues in dispute at the earliest possible date and test the accuracy and relevance of the facts advanced in support of their respective claims.

At the second stage, the parties will stress the merits of their claims and probe for weaknesses in the other side's contentions. They will advance express or implied threats of what they will do if they fail to get what they want and promises of what they will do if they do get what they want. Silence and body language accompanying the words may often send meaningful messages. Up to this point, the negotiations will have consisted almost entirely of words with no overt actions accompanying the threats and promises.

The Crunch: A Point of No Return

The third and final stage in the life cycle of a conflict is best played out against a deadline or what is sometimes called the crunch: that point in a negotiation when no decision becomes a decision. Until the crunch, the parties will most often hesitate before making any significant changes in their position. There is little risk before the crunch in making no decision. The crunch signals that the time for decision-making has arrived with rewards for the right decision and penalties for the wrong one.

The crunch was clearly in force on the day before the long and bitter basketball lockout was settled on Wednesday, January 6, 1999. The owners had threatened to cancel the season the next day if the union failed to accept their so-called "final" offer. The union's executive committee had scheduled a vote of the membership on Wednesday. Acceptance would have ended the strike in a defeat for the union that would leave the players divided and disgruntled and hardly in a mood to do their best for the owners. A rejection of the offer would likely have ended the season with the dispute still unresolved. The dire consequences of what the next day would bring precipitated an all night-session and a final agreement both sides enthusiastically ratified.

John L. Lewis, the skillful leader of the United Mine Workers and founder of the Committee for Industrial Organizations (CIO), demonstrated that he thoroughly understood the value of the crunch. In bargaining collectively on the terms of successor agreements, he would invariably say "no contract, no work," meaning that if an agreement was not reached by the termination day of the existing collective bargaining, his members would immediately strike. Based on past experience, the operators as well as the miner workers knew that Lewis meant what he said.

His strike threat provided both sides with an incentive to reach an agreement by the date the contract expired. If it took place, the mines would be shut down and the miners would be out of work. Most times, agreements were reached before the deadline, the crunch date.

The Unusual Crunch that Ended the 1998 Strike at General Motors

An unusual crunch hastened settlement of strikes of 49 and 56 days at two GM plants in Flint, Michigan in the late spring and early summer of 1998: the fear that both sides shared was the outcome of an arbitration hearing that had just been completed. The arbitrator had to make a decision within 30 days but could make it at any time before the deadline. The strike had idled nearly 200,000 GM employees in plants dependent on parts made in the two struck plants. The strike ultimately cost GM $3 billion in sales and $2 billion in profits and the employees $1 billion in lost wages.

GM initiated the arbitration under the terms of its national collective bargaining agreement with the UAW. As is usual in labor-management relationships, the agreement prohibited strikes or lockouts during its term and provided for arbitration of disputes arising under that agreement.

But GM and the UAW also have agreements with locals of the union covering matters specifically related to the local plants. These agreements also prohibit strikes and lockouts and require arbitration. However, they permit strikes or lockouts in disputes over three issues: health and safety, contracting out and production standards. These issues are of such monumental importance to both sides that they prefer to resort to self-help rather than let an arbitrator decide them.

The UAW claimed that the strikes at the two Michigan plants were over one or more of the issues that permitted strikes in lieu of arbitration. GM disagreed, contending that the UAW was using the local strikes to force settlement of national issues that could only be addressed when the current national agreement expired in September of 1999. The permanent arbitrator under the contract, Tom Roberts, was asked to decide whether the strike was local or national in scope. If he decided in favor of GM, the strike could be enjoined. If he decided that the strike was legal, he might open the door to extended use of local strikes on issues affecting all plants.

As the arbitration hearing drew to a close, it became evident that neither GM nor the UAW wanted to run the risk of an adverse decision. Their joint fear of what the arbitrator might decide created the crunch that precipitated the settlement. If they did not settle the dispute, the arbitrator's award could have led either to an injunction banning the strike or an intensified conflict. Both sides had too much at stake to let an arbitrator make the decision for them. Undoubtedly, they will be arguing over how to draw the line between national and local disputes during the 1999 negotiations over a new agreement. In all probability, they will work out a compromise on the issue.

Open Covenants, Secretly Arrived At

In an address to Congress on January 8, 1918, President Woodrow Wilson spelled out 14 points for our postwar peace negotiations. The first and most noteworthy was: "Open covenants of peace, openly arrived at." But the reality is that open covenants secretly arrived at is the regular practice in most major negotiations. It can be venal if the results are not made public, but not if they are released in timely fashion.

In negotiations in the automobile industry on successor bargaining agreements, the negotiators usually flood the media with press releases at the onset of their talks. They are designed not for their opponents in the negotiation but mainly to influence and inform the employees as well as the public.

At an appropriate point in the talks, both sides will usually impose a news blackout on their talks. That is a sure sign that they are getting down to business and often a sign that they are near an agreement.

The Bargaining Table, Where Is It?

We tend to speak of negotiation as taking place at the bargaining table just as we assume that professional baseball and football are played in a stadium. But negotiation can take place anywhere and at any time. When the negotiators are together, where they sit at the bargaining table can be important. But they need not be in the same room for negotiations to be taking place. They can negotiate by telephone, fax or e-mail. Even in the absence of discussions, the parties can be negotiating. Not responding to a proposal may sometimes be impolite. But it can also be a bargaining ploy, in effect a statement advanced by not making one.

At the beginning of the Vietnam peace talks in Paris in the early 1970s, a dispute erupted over the shape of the table. One side wanted a square table. The other said the table should be round. It sounded silly, but was relevant to whether the Vietcong and the South Vietnamese would be recognized as participants in their own right or simply as cohorts of the North Vietnamese and the United States.

In many negotiations, the bargaining table is simply where the parties exchange proposals and information, with major decisions frequently made in executive sessions away from the table. Detractors sometimes call them secret meetings to imply that there is something sinister about them. Others refer to them as executive sessions.

The formal sessions of the peace talks on Vietnam were conducted at the Hotel Majestic in Paris. But the real negotiations were taking place in undisclosed locations. The talks at the hotel were simply a façade. That was evident from the fact that they were open to the public. I attended one of the sessions in researching an article I was writing on the peace talks. I watched the delegates alternate in reading statements prepared in advance by their principals. If either side suggested any new approach, the other side would surely not respond until authorized to do so. But long before they could respond, the media would have disseminated the statements they read throughout the world. Quite evidently, negotiations were not taking place in the so-called peace talks open to the public.

A representative of the North Vietnamese, whom I interviewed for my article on the negotiations, subsequently confirmed that there were secret talks going on. He incidentally mentioned that at one of the meetings he complimented Henry Cabot Lodge, the U.S. negotiator, on how well he looked. "I ride a stationary bicycle every day," Lodge told him. The representative claimed that he then turned to one of his associates and whispered, "No wonder we're not getting anywhere."

Any sophisticated negotiator would quickly acknowledge that meetings open to the public are hardly the way to conduct meaningful negotiations. The obvious purpose of both sides in conducting their talks in public view was mainly to impress their respective constituencies with their efforts to end the war. If anything, their exchanges in public were proof that discussions to end the war were taking place in secret somewhere else.

The Spokesmen at the Bargaining Table

"As two men ride of a horse," Shakespeare wrote in *Much Ado About Nothing,* "one must ride behind." In negotiation, there are two horses to ride: one for the individual who is the chief spokesman for his side and the other for the individual or individuals who are the chief decision-makers. The rider on both horses can be but is not necessarily the same individual.

In labor-management negotiations, the company's chief executive officer is usually the chief decision-maker. But he rarely comes to the bargaining table. The director of labor-management relations usually acts as the company's chief spokesman. The union's chief spokesman at the bargaining table is generally a top official of the labor organization. He is frequently at the bargaining table. A committee of shop officials usually accompanies him. But almost invariably any agreement they reach must be submitted to the rank-and-file for ratification.

Companies and unions can have fierce battles over wages and other conditions of employment. But they almost always wind up with an agreement. In most cases, they cannot exist without each other. I have been present at the conclusion of many collective bargaining disputes at which the "mortal enemies" of a few days earlier have smilingly announced the happy ending of their bitter battle.

There are vast differences between on-going relationships in which the parties must continue to live with each other and disputes growing out of first and last time negotiations in which the disputants are unlikely to see each other ever again. In one-shot dealings, the focus is primarily on the present. In on-going situations, the past informs and shapes the present and often the future.

Individual Versus Representative Negotiations

An individual can negotiate for himself or retain someone to negotiate for him. In either event, he is the final decision-maker. If he is negotiating for himself, he has no need to consult with anyone else. If he has retained a lawyer or consultant, he can easily communicate with his representative.

In negotiations involving group entities, such as corporations, unions and government agencies, the negotiation takes on an entirely different complexion. Groups have no separate corporeal existence. They are inanimate entities created by individuals pursuant to laws and they can only act through individuals who make the group's negotiating decisions. Group decisions can be made in concert with two or more decision-makers. They are sometimes made by a single individual.

If made by more than a single individual, the decision-makers will argue with each other on what they should do. Their aim, of course, is to design the strongest bargaining position for their side. Their discussions are, nonetheless, a form of negotiation that precedes and sometimes tracks the main negotiations. As a result, there is often a negotiation going on not only between the disputants at the bargaining table but also between and among the decision-makers away from the table.

In whatever way the group arrives at its decisions, the wishes of the individual or individuals who make the decisions are usually carried out by officials of the group or outsiders retained to represent them.

A representative in negotiation derives his authority from his principal and must necessarily consult with his principal on goals and strategies and the scope of his authority before the negotiations begin. All of these factors may be, and are usually, reassessed and modified as the negotiation progresses to its conclusion.

A negotiator's prime objective is to get the best deal for his principal. But he is simultaneously vying for his principal's approval. It is not only important for him to get the best deal for his side but also to satisfy his principal that he has gotten the best deal. I once asked a negotiator which he would prefer: the very best deal his principal could expect on condition that his principal would not know that he had negotiated the deal, or one that was not as good but would eminently please his principal who would know that he was responsible for its achievement. Before he could answer, I suggested that he take the Fifth Amendment.

A negotiator in a representative capacity is frequently asked by his opponents if he has authority to make a deal. He will want to say that he has such authority. If he says that he is not authorized to conclude a final agreement, his opponent might respond by claiming that there is no reason for him to negotiate with a representative lacking authority to conclude an agreement.

This may be a neat bargaining ploy but it is not well founded in actual practice. A negotiator claiming full authority to bind a principal usually overstates the case. No negotiator is ever authorized to give the store away and will surely think twice before reaching an agreement his principal might disapprove.

Regardless of what authority a negotiator in a representative capacity possesses, he will almost invariably check with the ultimate decision-maker before making a final commitment. Nor is there any reason for him to be apologetic about consulting his principal. His opponent will assume that he has to get final authorization from the ultimate decision-maker whether he admits it or not.

The officials of group entities may be empowered to make final decisions. The ultimate principals on the side of the companies are the stockholders. They are rarely consulted during the course of negotiations of major corporations. They have their say at the annual meeting, when the stockholders elect directors. But unions of all sizes are generally required to enter into tentative agreements subject to the ratification of their members. As their leaders negotiate, they will constantly reflect on what they believe will be acceptable to their constituents—the final decision-makers.

It can be a matter of great embarrassment to a negotiator if his membership rejects an agreement he has negotiated and recommended for ratification. Whitney M. Young, the personable executive director of the National Urban League before his untimely death, was constantly concerned about getting out of touch with the wishes of his members. "I would hate," he once told me in a discussion on group leadership, "to find myself saying there goes my followship." Both Mr. Netanyahu and Mr. Arafat faced determined opposition among members of their constituencies to the agreement they reached under President Clinton's auspices.

Negotiation and the Media

Conflict resolution is an exercise in communications. While the parties mainly communicate directly with each other, they can communicate through a mediator or use the media to send signals, float trial balloons, convey threats and promises and project bargaining strength as well as a determination to hold fast. In disputes involving groups with large constituencies such as publicly held companies, unions, political organizations, governmental agencies and special interest groups, the parties can and do use the media to communicate with their constituents as well as their opponents.

Dealing with the media is itself a form of negotiation requiring specialized skills including knowledge of how the media works. Some negotiators find it useful to engage public relations consultants to assist them in communications with and through the media.

Many disputants and most companies prefer to keep complex negotiations away from the glare of public scrutiny. They may be sensitive to publicity or concerned about untimely or untoward disclosures that might impair their bargaining position. The media may be after information that might embarrass one side or the other. The comments of respected publications can sometimes influence the outcome, especially if they pass judgment on the issues in dispute.

In high-profile disputes, reporters will usually press the negotiators for information on the status of the negotiations. In their anxiety to get insider information, reporters may sometimes write stories that create questions that can be troublesome for the negotiators.

For bargaining reasons, a negotiator may take a position which he is prepared to change at the right time. Obviously, he will be unwilling to disclose his ultimate strategy to the media. When pressed to give answers that are relevant to their bargaining positions, negotiators with any experience will look for ways of avoiding an answer. They should be careful not to mislead the media while trying to avoid answering questions they will have to address at the bargaining table. Michael J. Quill, president of the transit workers union, was not known for the modesty of his initial demands. On one occasion, a reporter asked him if he would settle for a dollar less. "Not one penny less," was his emphatic reply. The final settlement was significantly less.

After giving the media sketchy information about what had taken place during an all night session, I have sometimes been asked why it took so long to accomplish so little. My inconclusive answer hardly satisfied the media. But the absence of little that is newsworthy at the end of a long session is not proof by itself that there hasn't been progress. For one thing, the dispute is a day closer to its final denouement. For another, the parties may have gotten a better understanding of the obstacles they face in reaching an agreement. In many cases, the parties may have made more progress than they realize.

In a major dispute involving the Newspaper Guild, which includes reporters among its members, a prominent newswriter who had dropped by the union's meeting place was horrified to find the negotiators sitting around and playing cards. Actually, they were waiting for a response from the publisher and were just as well off playing cards as talking about the weather. There are such dry spells in complex negotiations and it is not unusual for negotiators to mark time until they are either called upon to engage directly in talks with the other side or to deliberate on how to respond to new developments.

Tacit Negotiations: Cuomo Versus Clinton

Negotiations can be conducted through express, implied or even tacit exchanges. Tacit negotiations can sometimes solve a problem the parties cannot easily negotiate face-to-face. They may have solved a negotiation between President Clinton and Governor Mario M. Cuomo on his possible appointment to the Supreme Court.

For the purposes of this illustration, which is largely based on surmise, I am assuming that Cuomo, a lawyer and former law professor and then Governor of New York, wanted President Clinton to appoint him to the United States Supreme Court to fill the seat occupied by Justice White and that the President was not keen on naming him— even though he had said during the 1992 campaign that Cuomo was superbly qualified. For months after the vacancy occurred, Clinton took no action, leading to my assumption that he did not want to name Cuomo but was unsure how to avoid making that appointment.

Clinton's silence became even more enigmatic as the Washington press corps continued to describe Cuomo as the leading contender for the opening. After months of indecision, it was reported that the President tried to contact Governor Cuomo on March 29, but that the Governor did not finally speak with Clinton until the night of April 1.

Neither the White House nor Cuomo disclosed the content of their discussion, but it is probable that the President did not offer Cuomo the appointment because he wanted to keep open his option to appoint someone else.

The media also reported that in their conversation, Cuomo told the President that he did not wish to be considered for the vacancy. He confirmed his withdrawal in a letter he sent the President on April 7 and released to the press at that time.

But there was speculation, according to the *New York Times,* that Cuomo may have withdrawn his name after sensing or learning that he was unlikely to receive the nomination. Cuomo rejected that interpretation by saying in his letter of April 7 that he did not know whether the President might name him to the Court; the White House backed him up on this point.

Clinton's failure for months to make a clear decision on Cuomo's appointment was surely a tacit signal that he had doubts. Cuomo is a very sensitive man. It is fair to assume that the selection of another candidate would cause him embarrassment that he would not suffer lightly.

It is also logical to assume that the President was reluctant to embarrass Cuomo. In the meantime, Clinton and Cuomo were tacitly communicating with each other. Cuomo finally got the message. He accepted the result as gracefully as he could by withdrawing his name from consideration. Tacit negotiations had resolved their negotiation.

CHAPTER THREE

THE DYNAMICS OF NEGOTIATION

THERE are no simple tricks one can quickly learn to win victories in negotiations. Nevertheless, one can become more proficient by understanding and practicing the key elements. There are many useful books and courses on conflict resolution, including some specifically on negotiation. For the most part, they are designed to teach people how to beat their opponents.

I recently received a brochure for a one-day seminar entitled "How to Be a 'Tough-As-Nails' Negotiator." It contains some intriguing topics on what you can expect to learn: "Assembling an Arsenal of Negotiating Skills, Plotting a Plan of Attack, Deploying Your Hardball Techniques and Forcing Your Opponent to Surrender."

There are times when a tough-as-nails approach will work. But the basic aim of negotiation is to get your opponent to agree to give you what you want. You may be able to bully him into doing that. You can also be successful by being skillfully persuasive. Pounding the table and shouting is not by itself a mark of smart negotiation.

In 1937, a man named Dale Carnegie wrote *How to Win Friends and Influence People*. It became a best-seller, with a variety of principles and many examples on making friends and influencing people. Carnegie advanced nine principles that are as useful in negotiation as they are in influencing people to give you what you want:

1. Begin with praise and honest appreciation.
2. Call attention to people's mistakes indirectly.
3. Talk about your own mistakes before criticizing the other person.
4. Ask questions instead of giving direct orders.
5. Let the other person save face.
6. Praise the slightest improvement and praise every improvement. Be "hearty in your approbation and lavish in your praise."

7. Give the other person a fine reputation to live up to.

8. Use encouragement. Make the fault seem easy to correct.

9. Make the other person happy about doing the thing you suggest.

Carnegie also mentions three "fundamental techniques" that are equally as useful in negotiation as they are in making friends: don't "criticize, condemn or complain" about the person you are trying to influence; express "honest and sincere appreciation" of what he does or says; and arouse in him an "eager want" to do what you are proposing. But negotiation involves far more than merely pleasing your opponent. It is an interactive contest of communications that depends heavily on the way people react to each other.

The Right to Disagree

Since agreement is usually the stated objective of both sides in a negotiation, the possibility of disagreement is always present. Indeed, for a true negotiation to exist, both sides must possess the right to disagree as well as to agree.

But the existence of the right of both sides to disagree is not proof that they have equal bargaining strength. Yes, a skillful negotiator may be able to move an obstinate opponent to concessions, but not if the opponent's inherent bargaining strength is patently superior.

Jack Benny, who projected himself on radio and television as a dedicated tightwad, proved how tight he was when he hesitated on stage before answering an assailant who demanded his money or his life. After a long pause, Benny said, "I'm thinking!" His assertion of bargaining strength drew loud laughs.

A fundraiser seeking a contribution from a prospective donor has little bargaining strength if he is turned down. He can only rely on his ingenuity. Whitney Young successfully tested his bargaining strength by returning a substantial check the president of an automobile company had sent him as a contribution to the National Urban League.

"You are too good a friend," he told the executive, "for me to allow you to be embarrassed by the size of your contribution compared with those of your competitors." A significantly larger check with a note of thanks was promptly dispatched.

A landlord with a waiting list of applicants for apartments has little to lose if a tenant refuses to meet his price, as I recently learned.

The Exploitation of Potential Force

A negotiator's bargaining strength can vary with an opponent's impression of the strength he possesses, whether real or feigned. A negotiator's ability to project bargaining strength, which he may or may not possess, depends on many things. It is a skill a negotiator may inherently possess or gain through experience.

In his book *The Strategy of Conflict,* Professor Schelling of Harvard describes the "threat" to do something that will induce your opponent to give you what you want as "the exploitation of potential force." The term is well chosen.

A threat is invariably less expensive and often far more useful than its exercise. It succeeds if both sides believe that it will take place and that there is no workable alternative. But the threat can be costly if it has to be exercised.

The threat by the 15,000 air traffic controllers to strike gave them bargaining leverage they lost when they actually walked off the job and were replaced at President Reagan's order. The controllers apparently assumed that Reagan, whom they had supported in the 1980 election, would settle quickly. But federal law prohibits the employment of anyone who participates in a strike against the government. Even so, the President took a tremendous risk in replacing virtually all of the regular controllers on such short notice. Had there been an air crash, he probably would have been blamed. But the President had little choice. In pursuance of the law, he gave the controllers 48 hours to return to work and then filled their jobs with replacements. The controllers not only lost the strike; almost all of them lost their jobs.

The law prohibiting strikes in federal employment has no counterpart in the private sector. But a 1938 Supreme Court decision permits employers in an economic strike to hire strike replacements and promise them permanent employment. The decision remained largely dormant for many years. It came into active use after the air traffic controllers' dramatic defeat.

Force: A Prime Component of Bargaining Strength

Legally or illegally applied, force is a component of bargaining strength. It can take many forms. Simply saying no is an assertion of force.

Force that is permissible varies with the circumstances of each case. There may be times when a frustrated negotiator in the private sector relishes the thought of using force to pressure a recalcitrant opponent into submission. But he is limited by law, morals and practicality and usually restrains himself before yielding to the temptation.

It differs in the affairs of nations. UN Secretary-General Kofi Annan was quoted as saying, "You can do a lot with diplomacy." He added, however, "You can do a lot more with diplomacy backed up by firmness or force."* Firmness can include economic sanctions as an alternative to war. They worked effectively in South Africa. War, whether declared or not, is the ultimate expression of force in foreign affairs. It is an option most nations prefer not to use.

But there may be circumstances in foreign affairs when there is no other alternative. As the leading power of the world, the United States is frequently called upon to resolve disputes that threaten or breach world peace, international agreements or human rights. There is no doubt that we possess the power to use force for such purposes. The situations involving Bosnia, Israel and the Palestinians, Iraq and Ireland are good examples. In several of these conflicts, we have used force. We formally declared war on Iraq for invading Kuwait. President Bush had our armed forces invade Panama to capture the head of that nation and bring him to the United States to stand trial for his misdeeds.

We have also threatened to use force which, as I have said, has been called the exploitation of potential force.

President Clinton belatedly and reluctantly used force to bring the Bosnian Serbs to the bargaining table in Dayton, Ohio, as Richard Holbrooke so graphically describes in his book *To End A War.* Holbrooke played a leading role in settling the differences between and among the warring factions in Bosnia and won plaudits for helping to persuade our government to approve renewed bombing of the Serbs.

Holbrooke calls the relations between force and diplomacy the "classic" dilemma in political-military affairs. "It is now essential," he declared as the issue of renewed bombing was being debated, "to establish that we are negotiating [not mediating] from a position of strength" and that "[i]f the air strikes resume and hurt the negotiations, so be it."

---

*As I observed in Chapter One, diplomacy is defined as the art and practice of conducting negotiations between nations.

But the decision to use force is far from an easy one for civilized nations to make as revealed by President Clinton's on-again, off-again threat to bomb Iraq for Saddam Hussein's repeated violations of the UN resolution on arms inspection. In the confrontation that came to a head in November of 1998, a last-minute settlement posed a question that was answered differently in Baghdad and Washington. A front-page news analysis in the *New York Times* was headlined: "Who Backed Down?"

As the leading power in the world, the United States is in a unique position. The limitations on the exercise of force that govern the actions of negotiators in the private sector are hardly comparable to those that face the United States in the exercise of its worldwide responsibilities. But there are restraints that our leaders must take into account.

When Saddam Hussein continued his defiance, Clinton bombed Iraq the day before the House of Representatives was to vote on impeaching him. Some of his opponents argued that it was a ploy to forestall the impeachment proceedings. Undoubtedly Clinton and his advisers had reflected on the possibility his action might be seen as more politically than militarily motivated. The political consequences of such situations are themselves a restraining influence.

Litigation and the Threat to Sue

Litigation is the bedrock of our system of conflict resolution. The courts are open to anyone who elects to resolve a claim by suing. As I have previously mentioned, a claimant does not have to get his opponent's consent to sue him. He will, of course, face the delays and costs of our court systems. The threat to sue, however, is relatively inexpensive. It is frequently used to induce negotiations. As a matter of fact, far more lawsuits are settled than the courts decide.

If a claimant can't get the other side to sit down and talk, he may have no alternative but to sue. A lawyer retained by a client will almost always send a letter announcing his intention to sue but add that he and his client would be available to discuss settlement in order to avoid the costs of litigation. The cost of litigation is often taken into account in the negotiation of a settlement.

Some aggressive advocates use publicity to embarrass their opponent. It is often used for that purpose in high profile matrimonial disputes. Publicity is also used to enlist support in class action disputes or hostile takeover contests. There is, however, a growing tendency on the part of the courts to frown on litigation accompanied by publicity. Used properly, with or without publicity, a threat to sue can be a perfectly legitimate tactic in bargaining situations.

A threat to sue reported in the *New York Times* presented some of the questions I have posed. It involved a claim by Irina Shchukin over ownership of a collection of 450 paintings, including many by modern masters. The paintings had been left behind in Russia by her late father, the textile millionaire Sergei I. Shchukin, when he fled to France in 1918 in the wake of the Bolshevik Revolution. Later that year, Lenin's new government nationalized the paintings, which were eventually divided between the permanent collections of the Hermitage in St. Petersburg and the Pushkin Museum in Moscow. At the time that the story appeared in print, fourteen Matisses from the collection were on loan to the Georges Pompidou Center in Paris, where they were on exhibition.

Mlle. Shchukin, in her 70s and living in the south of France, wrote a letter to Russian President Boris Yeltsin claiming that the Matisses and the rest of the collection were rightfully the property of her family and requesting that they be returned.

She also offered to donate them to Russia, provided that the whole collection was housed in Moscow's Troubetskoy Palace and identified as a Shchukin family donation. She included one other proviso: that her family receive some compensation for the collection. The letter was a clear invitation to Yeltsin to negotiate. As you might imagine, Yeltsin (or whoever handled the matter) could see that Mlle. Shchukin was threatening to sue and embarrass the Russians. No reply was given.

As soon as she realized that her letter would not elicit a reply, Mlle. Shchukin turned to the family's lawyer, Bernard Jouanneau, who promptly issued a public statement asserting that unless the Russians agreed to negotiate, Mlle. Shchukin *intended* to bring a lawsuit asserting ownership whenever any painting from the collection traveled outside Russia. As far as we know, the press release produced no response from the Russians. But it did make an impression on Marion Julien, an official of the Pompidou Center, who announced that if any court decision were to throw doubt on Russia's ownership of the paintings, it would certainly discourage Russian museums from lending the works for exhibition abroad.

Mlle. Shchukin's plight demonstrates the difficulty of trying to negotiate with a party that has little or no interest in reaching an agreement. Her letter to Yeltsin was an appropriate first step. But it is easy to understand why he failed to respond; with all his other problems, it is likely he never even saw her letter. Her attorney's public threat to sue the Russian government just as the Matisses were going on display in Paris was handled with finesse. It attracted the attention of the Pompidou Center. Perhaps the lawyer encouraged the publicity.

Negotiation is a game of communication, and so it is not unusual for negotiators, including lawyers and labor leaders and company officials, to communicate through the media. It does not appear that the mere threat to sue was sufficient to induce the Russians to open negotiations with Mlle. Shchukin. Regardless, it was a good try.

Credibility, Earned and Lost

Establishing and maintaining a reputation for credibility is perhaps the most important asset a negotiator can possess. In one-shot negotiations, one's general reputation can enhance or detract from his credibility. In on-going relationships, credibility is measured by what has been done in the past. Credibility can also be earned or lost through performance.

In a negotiation in which I was involved, the chief negotiator on one side was ready to advance what he wanted the other side to believe was positively his final offer. He rehearsed what he was to say and how he should say it. To emphasize the finality of his proposal, he was told to stand while speaking and then leave the room immediately after. He did well in rehearsal and even better on stage, up to the very last moment. Then he forgot. Instead of leaving the room, he sat down. His continued presence was immediately construed as a readiness to resume negotiating.

Was Rupert Murdoch's Threat Credible?

In 1988, Rupert Murdoch, the international media mogul, agreed to sell the *New York Post* for $37.6 million to Peter Kalikow, a real estate developer. But there was a condition. Kalikow insisted that $24 million in savings be achieved in negotiations with the nine unions representing the *Post*'s employees before he would take title.

Aware that the unions were unlikely to agree to any savings in the absence of a deadline for decision-making (a "crunch" date, as I discussed in Chapter Two), Murdoch announced that he would shut the *Post* down if the unions had not agreed to the $24 million in savings by

2:30 on the afternoon of February 19, 1988. Patrick Purcell, the publisher of the *Post,* sought to enhance Murdoch's bargaining position by telling the unions that Murdoch had a reputation on three continents for carrying out his threats and that he would lose more in face than the value of the *Post* if he did not follow through with his threat to close the *Post* if they did not agree. The unions were concerned. Murdoch did have a reputation for carrying out the threats he made in negotiations. Was his current threat real or feigned?

The crunch date arrived all too soon. By that time, the unions had agreed to $22 million in savings. I was present at the meeting as the unions' advisor as they speculated on whether Murdoch would shut the *Post* down for the $2 million difference.

The president of the typesetters was the first to speak. His members, he said, had lifetime guarantees granted in 1974 in exchange for the elimination of all workrule restrictions on productivity and that he could not run the risk of losing the guarantees on the chance that Murdoch did not mean what he said.

The president of the pressmen's union spoke next. His members at New York's three largest newspapers, he explained, would have to vote on the settlement at the *Post* since his union's contract with the three papers, which included the *New York Times* and the *New York Daily News* as well as the *Post,* had a so-called "me-too"* provision that entitled the *Times* and *News* to the same concessions the pressmen were being asked to give the *Post.* His members at those papers, he emphasized, would surely vote against a cut in their pay to save the *Post.* Even worse, they would then unleash on him their fury over the mere suggestion that they vote to cut their pay regardless of the purpose. "I must," he added, "vote against giving Murdoch any additional concessions."

The stereotypers took the same position and most of the unions with similar "me-too" provisions were ready to join the pressmen and the stereotypers. Since any one union could prevent the deal from going through, George E. McDonald, the president of the Allied Printing Trades Council, the umbrella association of the autonomous unions of New York's printing trades, proposed that the unions vote unanimously to oppose the additional $2 million cut in pay. That is what they did.

---

*Me-too is the name borrowed from the universal pratice of children, but not confined to them, to cry "me-too" whenever any of their peers got something they thought they also deserved. Other examples of "me-tooism" are mentioned elsewhere in this book.

Soon after Murdoch was invited to meet with the unions in the hotel conference room they were occupying and I was asked to advise Murdoch that the unions would not give the additional $2 million. I delivered the message and then waited with everyone present to hear whether Murdoch would carry out his threat to shut the *Post* down.

After reflecting for a few tense moments, Murdoch turned to me and asked, "What do you propose?" He had blinked.

I suggested that he ask Kalikow to join the meeting. Murdoch said he could not, since his deal with Kalikow called for $24 million in savings. Murdoch's media advisor, Howard Rubenstein, then suggested that McDonald call Governor Cuomo and ask him to ask Kalikow to join the meeting. McDonald agreed and I accompanied McDonald with Murdoch and Rubenstein to a pay phone in the hallway.

When McDonald said he didn't know the Governor's number, Rubenstein was ready with it and the union leader dialed the number. The Governor answered the phone and quickly agreed to call Kalikow who said that he would discuss the proposal with his advisors and get back to the Governor.

About an hour later, Kalikow called to say that he would join the negotiations only if and when the nine unions agreed to the $24 million in savings. Ever resourceful, Murdoch quickly told the unions that, in recognition of their cooperation, he would contribute the extra $2 million out of his share of the purchase price. And that is how the conflict was resolved.

Murdoch's performance was skillful. Whether instinctive or planned, Murdoch's moves at every turn in the talks were on target. The unions were fearful that he would shut the paper down. But they could not accept the additional concessions he was demanding because of the impact on their many more members at the *Times* and *Daily News*. Even though he failed to get the remaining $2 million, Murdoch salvaged his multi-million dollar deal with Kalikow, who subsequently lost between $10 to $20 million a year running the *Post* or approximately $80 million according to newspaper accounts, and landed in bankruptcy as a result.*

---

*Thereafter, Murdoch reacquired the Post by merely assuming its liabilities. Knowledgeable viewers thought it was more of an ego trip than a sound investment. Time will tell. As of this writing, the *Post* and *News* are locked in a battle for survival. Whatever the motivation for the continued existence of the two newspapers, the readers are the beneficiaries of the determination of their publishers to keep them alive.

Negotiation: A Game of Hide-and-Seek and Puff-and-Bluff

In one sense, negotiation is a game of hide-and-seek. Both sides try to hide their ultimate intentions—their "reservation price" as it is sometimes called—while simultaneously probing to discover the other side's bottom line.

Negotiation is a game of puff-and-bluff since negotiators regularly brag about the wares or services they are offering while downplaying any of their shortcomings. But they are prohibited from making any material false or misleading statements on which the other side might rely. Such statements can lead to court charges of fraud.

It is not always easy to distinguish between legitimate puffing-and-bluffing about products or services and misrepresentations about material facts the courts will condemn. Many court cases have turned on the line between a good argument and outright fraud.

But there is no law prohibiting a negotiator from misleading his opponent on what he will accept in settlement, as long as he does not make any false statements of facts on which his opponent might rely. He can say "I've made my final offer" when in fact he is prepared to go further. But he can't say that he has received a higher offer from someone else if that is untrue. What it comes down to is the difference between statements about intentions and statements of facts. The former can be false without being actionable; the latter, if proven, can be the basis for a lawsuit.

I once heard Mike Quill, the audacious president of the Transport Workers Union, swear he would never settle without a four-day week—a ridiculous demand, as he well knew. At the moment of truth, he agreed to drop the demand. When a reporter asked why he had abandoned his insistence on a four-day week after vowing he would never settle without it, Quill's quick reply was "Common sense, next question." No one, including the media, was shocked or surprised.

Bargaining in Good Faith

A disputant may come to the bargaining table with no real intention of reaching an agreement. As the saying goes, you can bring a horse to water but you cannot make him drink. Some negotiators may openly assert that they are "not negotiable" on one or more of the issues in dispute. A demand for unconditional surrender leaves no room for nego-

Ted Kheel and Mike Quill, president of the New York City
Transit Workers Union, discussing how to avoid a strike in
the 1940s.

tiation. It is by its terms non-negotiable. Some negotiators may go through the motions of negotiating, intending all the while to remain firmly opposed to any change in their position. Whether a negotiator admits it or not, he is non-negotiable if his mind is closed to change. It is difficult, however, to determine what is in a negotiator's mind. As a practical matter, he can only be judged by conduct including what he says or doesn't say.

As I have previously mentioned, collective bargaining is the specialized name of negotiation between labor and management. It is defined in the National Labor Relations Act as "the mutual obligation of the employer and the representative of the employees to meet at reasonable times and confer in *good faith* with respect to wages, hours and other terms and conditions of employment." I have not found the requirement of good faith in negotiation in any other law. Over the years, the National Labor Relations Board has issued many decisions interpreting the meaning of good faith. The board distinguishes between what it calls a *per se* violation of the law—a refusal to meet, for example—and a violation of good faith based on the overall behavior of the parties. The latter category depends on what is really in the mind of the negotiator, an exercise that a psychologist might be qualified to determine.

Boulwarism and Good Faith Bargaining

In a case in the 1960s involving a company named Fitzgerald Mills Corporation, the board and the courts had little trouble in concluding that the company had acted in bad faith after finding that the company's manager had said that "he would 'die and go to hell' before he would sign a contract and told his employees to 'get those union agitating sons of bitches' out of Fitzgerald."

But it is not nearly as easy to make such a finding when the parties are in fact negotiating with each other. The difficulty of passing judgment on the overall conduct of one of the parties was illustrated by the conflicting opinions of the judges in a landmark decision of the United States Court of Appeals Second Circuit in 1962. This decision upheld a ruling of the National Labor Relations Board finding that General Electric Company had failed to bargain in good faith with the International Union of Electrical, Radio, and Machine Workers, AFL-CIO.

The board's complaint charged that GE had violated its obligation to bargain in good faith in pursuing a plan its director of labor relations, Lemuel Boulware, had devised, which became known as Boulwarism in his honor. It was Boulware's response to the practice of unions demanding large increases at the onset of negotiations which the company countered by offering less than GE was ready to accept and then settling for the reasonable compromise it was prepared to offer in the first place. "Since we have to pay the bill," Boulware reasoned, "we want the employees to give us the credit for the increase."

Judge Irving R. Kaufman, who wrote the majority opinion holding that GE had not bargained in good faith, described Boulware's plan as threefold, beginning with GE soliciting comments from its local management personnel on the desires of the work force, and the type and level of benefits that they expected. These were then translated into specific proposals, and their cost and effectiveness researched, in order to formulate a "product" that would be attractive to the employees, and within the company's means. The last step, according to Judge Kaufman, was the most important, most innovative, and most often criticized. GE took its "product"—now a series of fully formed pro-posals—and "sold" it to its employees and the general public.

"Through a veritable avalanche of publicity, reaching awesome pro-portions prior to and during negotiations," Judge Kaufman wrote, "GE sought to tell its side of the issues to its employees. It described its pro-posals as a 'fair, firm offer,' characteristic of its desire to 'do right vol-untarily,' without the need for any union pressure or strike."

In negotiations, Judge Kaufman continued, GE announced that it would have nothing to do with the "blood-and-threat-and-thunder" approach, in which each side presented patently unreasonable demands, and finally chose a middle ground that both knew would be the probable outcome even before the beginning of the bargaining. The company believed, the Judge said, that such tactics diminished its cred-ibility in the eyes of its employees, and at the same time appeared to give the union credit for wringing from the company what it had been willing to offer all along. Henceforth, the Judge reported, GE would hold nothing back when it made its offer to the union, it would take all the facts into consideration, and make that offer it thought right under all the circumstances. Though willing to accept union suggestions based on facts the company might have overlooked, once the basic out-lines of the proposal had been set, the mere fact that the union dis-agreed would be no ground for change. When GE said firm, it meant firm, and it denounced the traditional give and take of the so-called auction bargaining as "flea bitten eastern type of cunning and dishon-est but pointless haggling."

In finding an "overall failure to bargain in good faith," Judge Kaufman was careful to say that the court was not deciding that "best offer first" bar-gaining technique was forbidden or that the court was requiring the employer to engage in "auction bargaining." Indeed, the National Labor Relations Act as amended specifically provides that the duty to bargain in good faith "does not compel either party to agree to a proposal or require the making of a concession."

In dissenting in part, Judge Henry Friendly complained that the majority had been quite explicit in describing what they were not deciding but that they were far less informative with respect to what they were deciding. The closest the lead opinion comes to this, Judge Friendly wrote, was its statement that "an employer may not so com-bine 'take-it-or- leave-it' bargaining methods with a widely publicized stance of unbending firmness that he is himself unable to alter a posi-tion once taken."

Judge Waterman challenged Judge Friendly's disssenting assertion that the standard Judge Kaufman set forth for determining overall good faith was vague or difficult to apply. "A company may make a firm, fair offer to the union and may stand by that offer, but the company should not be permitted to advertise to its employees that it believes in the firmness of its offers for the sake of firmness."

Taken together, the opinions confirm how difficult it is to determine whether a company or union that is participating in negotiations is or is not bargaining in good faith. As a practical matter, the ruling has had little effect. It can easily be countered by an employer or union going through the motions of bargaining in good faith regardless of their true intentions.

GE was not alone in seeking to win its employees' favor. The relationship of an employer and union doesn't end with the conclusion of the negotiations. The views and attitudes of the employees are of critical importance to the employer as well as the union. In recent times, companies have come to realize that the employees are the most relevant audience for them as well as for the unions. As a result, both sides in such situations are ever mindful of the impact their performance in bargaining will have on the employees.

Real or Feigned Negotiation in Selected Cases

Beginning in 1962 and continuing through 1991, I was directly involved in the resolution of virtually all of the labor disputes in New York City's newspapers—and there were many. The industry was changing dramatically as the computer was replacing hot type and as broadcast and cable television were challenging the print media. A half a dozen or more papers were forced out of business. The *New York Herald-Tribune*, which Horace Greeley founded in the early part of the nineteenth century, died under circumstances discussed below that put in question the publisher's true motive in negotiating with the unions.

The *New York Daily News*, which once possessed the largest circulation in the United States, was sold by its owner, the Tribune Company of Chicago, to Robert Maxwell under circumstances, also discussed below, that raised questions about the publisher's real objective.

In my opinion, neither of the publishers was keen on continuing their newspaper but both were reluctant to admit that they could not successfully run a newspaper in the most important media city in the world.

The Untimely Death of the New York Herald-Tribune

John Hay "Jock" Whitney, a shrewd investor, bought the *New York Herald Tribune* in 1958 for reasons unrelated to its quality as an investment. He acted at the urging of his friend, the publicist John Reagan "Tex" McCrary, whose aim was to keep the paper's voice of moderate Republicanism alive at a time when isolationism was intensifying in Middle America. It became evident, however, that Whitney was not ready to invest the money that would be required to make the *Tribune* a worthy competitor of the *Times*, its arch rival. The consequence of his ambivalence about investing in the paper was dramatically revealed at the time John Lindsay was about to announce that he was a candidate for Mayor. Whitney, as well as his newspaper, were actively supporting Lindsay's candidacy.

As Lindsay was pondering when to throw his hat in the ring, Robert Price, his campaign manager, offered to give the *Times* the announcement exclusively on condition that it would be run on the front page. A. M. Rosenthal, the managing editor, told Price that as a matter of principle the *Times* could not agree to any such condition. He added, however, that if the *Times* learned that an individual with Lindsay's qualifications had decided to run for Mayor, the *Times* would undoubtedly consider the story sufficiently newsworthy to report it on the front page. Price "leaked" the information to the *Times* and Clayton Knowles, a top political reporter, was assigned to write the story.

Knowing that it was difficult and costly for the *Tribune* to add new stories after nine o'clock in the evening, the *Times* withheld the story from its first edition. As soon as he was sure the *Tribune* could not copy the story from the *Times*, Knowles called Whitney at his home for comments on Lindsay's decision. The butler said that Mr. Whitney had retired.

"Please tell him when he wakes up," Knowles replied, "that John Lindsay is running for Mayor."

When Lindsay arrived at Whitney's office the next morning for a meeting on campaign financing and strategy, Whitney's fury could hardly be contained. But the deed was done. He was unwilling to invest in the equipment necessary for the *Tribune* to compete effectively with the *Times*.

At the end of the 1962-63 strike, which shut New York's papers down for 114 days, Walter Thayer, Whitney's designated publisher of the *Tribune,* asked me to join him in a meeting with the *Times* to discuss a merger of the two papers. Whitney had offered to sell the *Tribune* to the *Times* for one dollar on condition that the *Times* take over the newspaper, turn it into an afternoon paper, print both papers in its plant on 43rd Street and allow Whitney to be the publisher of the *Tribune* for the rest of his life. The *Tribune* would then be owned by the *Times* to do with as it pleased. The *Times* turned him down after a study indicated that it could not conveniently publish both newspapers in the same plant.

With Thayer's help, Whitney continued to hunt for a way to minimize his ownership of the *Tribune*. He courted a merger with Dorothy Schiff, then the owner of The Post, but nothing came of that. He finally succeeded in concluding a three-way merger with the *World-Telegram* and *Sun,* which was owned by Scripps-Howard, and the *New York Journal-American,* which Hearst owned. The original plan was to have the three newspapers become one afternoon paper. But Thayer convinced the owners of the other papers to allow Whitney to continue to publish the *Tribune* as a morning newspaper despite their belief that a morning paper could not succeed in competition with the *Times* and the *Daily News.* They were persuaded when Thayer agreed to cover any losses the morning paper sustained during a two-year trial period and to close the paper if it was not in the black at the end of the trial.

Publication of the new papers was delayed by inconclusive negotiations with the unions. As a result, the merged company ran out of the $4 million in cash and equipment and supplies that each of the three partners put up to launch the merger. To the surprise of his partners, Whitney refused to make any additional contributions. They went ahead without his support. It became obvious to me after a meeting I had with Whitney and Thayer that they had no interest in keeping the *Tribune* alive, but did not want the responsibility of throwing in the towel. The other two newspapers struggled on for several months and then gave up. The three newspapers died unceremoniously and Whitney was relieved of his commitment to moderate Republicanism.

The unions were identified as the culprits. But the real problem stemmed from the absence of sufficient market incentives to invest capital to replace out-dated equipment.

The Curious Sale of the Daily News

The *New York Daily News* was founded by the Tribune Company of Chicago in 1919 and became an instant success. It was run as a separate entity under the direction of Colonel Robert Patterson, a member of the founding family. The Tribune Company was delighted to keep hands off as long as profits were being sent to Chicago.

In the late seventies, Joseph F. Barletta, then the Manager of the *Daily News,* told Stanton R. Cook, the Tribune Company's president and CEO, that the newspaper was losing money and that its losses were likely to mount in the foreseeable future. I later learned that the Tribune Company had been told by its investment bankers, Salomon Brothers, that the company could not be taken public, as its officers desired, as long as the the *Daily News,* a principal holding, was losing money and destined to have its losses escalate.

Without acknowledging that there was anything wrong, the Tribune Company changed publishers and started an afternoon paper. But those and other measures didn't stop the losses. After losing some $20 million, the afternoon paper was dropped.

The new publisher, Robert Hunt, then turned to the unions for help. Together with George E. McDonald, the president of the association of newspaper unions, we advised Hunt that it was unlikely the unions would believe that the paper was in financial difficulties and that it would be wise for him to offer to allow the unions to designate an accountant to check the books. Hunt agreed provided that the unions' selected one of the big eight accounting firms and the firm agreed to sign a confidentiality statement. The unions accepted on condition that the *Daily News* pay the fee. With those matters out of the way, the unions chose Peat Marwick, then the largest of the big eight, and were persuaded that the *Daily News* was in trouble when Peat Marwick's representative met in executive session with the unions and convinced them that the newspaper was in serious financial trouble. Hunt then advised the unions that he had developed a restructuring plan and was flying to Chicago to obtain the Tribune Company's approval before submitting it to them.

Without notifying the unions in advance, the Tribune Company put the *Daily News* up for sale instead of approving Hunt's plan. But prospective buyers were turned off by the shutdown liabilities of the *Daily News,* estimated to be approximately $200 million. The Tribune Company then reversed course, took the *Daily News* off the market and turned back to the unions for help. To save the *Daily News,* the unions agreed to sufficient concessions for the Tribune Company to have a successful public offering. As part of the sale, the company's shares as split 500 to 1 were sold at a very favorable price. Its officials, who owned many of the shares as split, were among the principal beneficiaries.

Although the officials of the Tribune Company promised the unions that they would invest in a new plant and equipment, they never did. Instead they kept the *Daily News* alive by selling off many of its assets and seeking further concessions from the unions. With the passage of time, the *Daily News* again began to lose money. One option was to close the paper down. But if they did, the Tribune Company would likely be held liable for the shutdown liabilities. Besides, they were reluctant to admit that they could not run a successful newspaper in New York City.

In 1989, a new chief executive officer, Charles Brumback, replaced the amiable Stanton Cook. A former accountant, Brumback knew that something drastic had to be done. At his direction, the *Daily News* hired a Tennessee lawyer named Robert Ballow, who had a long record of success in defeating newspaper unions, and put him in sole charge of negotiating successor collective bargaining agreements with the ten unions. In a traditional formality, several unions authorized their leaders to strike if no agreement was reached. Ballow used this usual tactic as a pretext for advertising for "replacement" workers in the event of a strike, offering "permanent" employment to the replacements.

Thousands of unemployed workers responded and their names and addresses were duly recorded for future use. When the negotiations finally got under way, Ballow advanced demands that in effect asked the unions to waive their obligation to represent the interests of the employees on vital matters of concern. In a sense, Ballow was demanding that the unions agree to surrender unconditionally.

The *Daily News* also retained a public relations expert to help gain the support of the City's decision and opinion makers. He succeeded in placing an article in *Vanity Fair* many months before negotiations were scheduled to begin predicting that the *Daily News* would be at war with the unions.

He also distributed reams of information to political, social and religious leaders castigating the unions. Cardinal O'Connor was among the recipients. He investigated the information he had been given and wound up vigorously supporting the unions.

His Eminence Cardinal O'Connor being briefed by Kheel on developments in the 1990 lockout/strike at the New York Daily News.

As the negotiations progressed, it became clear that Ballow was determined to induce the employees to strike so that permanent replacements could be hired to fill their jobs. Recognizing that the Tribune Company had that plan in mind, the unions formally voted to avoid any action that might be construed a strike. The *Daily News* finally declared a minor plant dispute in the middle of the night a "strike," entitling the newspaper to fill the jobs of the so-called strikers with permanent replacements. Busloads of strike breakers were immediately dispatched to fill the jobs. Later, an administrative law judge of the National Labor Relations Board found that the *Daily News* had actually locked out its employees.

The bloody battle of the ten newspaper unions against the *Daily News* ended in 1991 when the Tribune Company sold the newspaper to Robert Maxwell for $60 million. An unusual aspect of the sale was that the seller paid the buyer the $60 million.

The explanation for this strange transaction can be found in the startling conclusion of a report the investment banking firm of Furman, Selz, Mager, Dietz & Birney issued in the middle of the battle, namely, that the stock of the Tribune Company would go up if the *Daily News* defeated the unions and that the stock would go up if the *Daily News* lost the battle. The author of the report had apparently based his conclusion on an interview with James Hoge, the newspaper's publisher. With this conclusion, Furman Selz had little hesitancy in advising its clients to buy the Tribune Company's stock. As soon as the unusual sale to Maxwell was announced, the Tribune Company's stock began moving up. By the time Maxwell took title to the *Daily News* on March 21, 1991, the Tribune Company's stock had appreciated by over a billion dollars.

Ironically, despite the commitment of permanent employment the *Daily News* gave the replacements, the Tribune Company authorized Maxwell to dismiss the replacements upon taking title to the newspaper. As the replacements left their jobs, they sabotaged the wiring in the main printing plant, which delayed the reopening of the *Daily News* for two days.

Unconditional Surrender Leaves No Room for Negotiation

A Chinese proverb cautions against attacking a square fortress on four sides. Leave one side open for retreat, it implies. The Allies insisted that Hitler surrender unconditionally. Nor would we bargain with the Japanese over their retention of their emperor before dropping the atom bomb on Hiroshima. President Bush did not demand that President Noriega of Panama agree to stand trial in the United States. He sent our armed forces to Panama and captured him. Nor did Bush insist on unconditional surrender to end our war against Iraq's invasion of Kuwait. It is doubtful that Saddam Hussein would have agreed regardless of the consequences.

Nevertheless, it is almost impossible to avoid some negotiation of a demand for an *agreement* to surrender unconditionally without exercising brute force.

When the United States insisted that the Haitian General Raul Cedras step down as President of Haiti and had bombers ready to enforce the demand, former President Jimmy Carter traveled to Haiti for discussions with the General. He was accompanied by Senator Sam Nunn of Georgia and former General Colin Powell. Word had it that they were under instructions from our State Department that there could be no negotiation on our insistence that the General resign and leave the country.

There is also some reason to believe that Nunn and Powell were sent along to make sure that Carter did not engage in any negotiations with General Cedras. But there were negotiations.

The points discussed included when Cedras would leave the country, what he could take with him, what would happen to the house he owned in Haiti, where he should go after leaving Haiti and who should pay for his expenses. The negotiated resolution of those issues facilitated compliance with our unconditional demand that he abdicate and leave the country.

TEN COMMANDMENTS FOR NEGOTIATORS

    I. Seek agreement on a clear definition of the issues in dispute at the earliest possible time.

    II. In keeping with the sentiment in the words of the eminent Scottish poet Robert Burns, try to see yourself as your opponent sees you.

    III. Try also to see your opponent as he sees himself.

    IV. False statements of material facts can be illegal. They are also unwise, especially in continuing relationships. As the Bible warns: "Bread of deceit is sweet to a man; but afterwards his mouth shall be filled with gravel."

    V. Puffing-and-bluffing about your products, services or bargaining intentions are permissible if they do not include false or misleading statements of material facts.

    VI. Credibility is key. It is earned or lost through performance. Take good care of it. It is invaluable.

    VII. Silence and body language can be as significant as words and deeds. Be as mindful of what you don't say and do as you are of what you do say and do.

    VIII. In negotiation, timing is critical. As the Bible tells us: "To everything there is a season, and a time to every purpose under the heaven" including "a time to keep silence, and a time to speak; a time to love, and a time to hate; a time of war, and a time of peace."

    IX. Keep cool. As the Bible also tells us, "A wrathful man stirreth up strife but he that is slow to anger appeaseth strife."

    X. Be ready for decision-making at the crunch. It is the time to put up or shut up.

CHAPTER FOUR

THE STRUCTURE OF MEDIATION

The Mediator's Role in Negotiations

NEGOTIATORS, mediators and arbitrators have the same goal—to resolve the dispute—but their incentives are not the same. The negotiator seeks to get the best deal for his side. The mediator is simply called upon to assist the disputants in agreeing with each other. He can't tell the disputants what to do. They remain in control of the outcome.

An arbitrator resolves disputes by making a decision based on the record presented to him. He weighs the facts and applies the relevant criteria of decision making. His authority to decide the dispute is the product of an agreement between the disputants. They set the stage on which the arbitrator acts. He succeeds if his decision is sound and not whether either side likes the decision.

The Mediator: Catalyst on a Hot Tin Roof

The publicist Tex McCrary succinctly summed up the duties of a mediator when he correctly observed that a mediator is a catalyst on a hot tin roof. William E. Simkin, longtime arbitrator and highly regarded director of the Federal Mediation and Conciliation Service, once—and perhaps more eloquently—described the personality of a mediator as one having

> ". . .the patience of Job, the sincerity and bulldog characteristic of the English, the wit of the Irish, the physical endurance of a marathon runner, the broken-field dodging abilities of a halfback, the guile of a Machiavelli, the confidence-retaining characteristics of a mute, the hide of a rhinoceros, and the wisdom of Solomon."

In the best of all possible negotiations, with the highest degree of competency on both sides and no extraneous roadblocks to the negotiation of an agreement, the parties themselves should be capable of reaching an agreement without the help of a mediator. The companies and unions in the automobile industry regularly refuse mediation and they have a pretty good track record of direct negotiations.

But it is not an admission of failure for disputants at impasse to seek or accept the assistance of a mediator. Even the most experienced negotiator can benefit from the presence of a mediator in settlement of a dispute. As I pointed out in Chapter Three, negotiation is a game of strategy in which the best course of action for each player depends on what the other player or players do. The mediator can assist the parties in keeping on the path to a settlement.

Mediation: An Art, not a Science

There are no formal rules of mediation and no standard procedures, although service providers such as the American Arbitration Association and the CPR Institute for Dispute Resolution provide guidelines for mediators and disputants. Some mediators are more effective in hard fought but simply defined conflicts, usually over money. Schelling refers to these as distributive disputes.

Others are more proficient in negotiations with complex issues requiring careful thought. Schelling calls the latter efficiency disputes.

Regardless of the type of dispute, the mediator must enjoy the confidence of both sides. This is not an easy challenge to meet. In effect, he has to be the friend of enemies. The mediator will not offend either side if he merely acts as a messenger. But he has to be more active to make a significant contribution in getting the parties to agree with each other.

It is imperative for a mediator to avoid any action or inaction that might strengthen or weaken the bargaining position of either party. Nor should he allow any opinion he may have of how the dispute should be resolved to influence his conduct in settling the dispute. His efforts should reflect the likely outcome of the dispute if both sides were negotiating at peak efficiency.

Mediation: A Profession or an Avocation?

Anyone can be a mediator, and many people volunteer to serve as mediators simply as a public service. No license is required. The same holds true for arbitration although an arbitrator's qualifications should parallel those of a judge. A select group of individuals, especially active in labor-management and commercial disputes have become professional arbitrators, devoting virtually all of their time to the resolution of disputes through arbitration.

Some years ago, a group of professional arbitrators formed an association called the Academy of Arbitrators. It seeks to protect, enhance and promote the profession and meets annually to discuss the critical issues the arbitrators are facing.

There are not as many individuals serving regularly as mediators. Nor is there a professional association of mediators comparable to the Academy of Arbitrators. There is, however, an overlap in the work and demand for mediators and arbitrators.

Since arbitrators as third party neutrals share the obligation of impartiality, they are sometimes asked to serve as mediators. They may also undertake to mediate during the course of arbitration.

But a good arbitrator is not necessarily a good mediator, and vice versa. The required skills are definitely not interchangeable.

Academics tend to make good arbitrators. They think clearly and adhere strictly to the rules. They are not always good as mediators. Instead of focusing on what both sides will accept, they tend to lean in the direction of what they think is right when they should be focusing on what will be acceptable to both sides.

The Mediator's Strength Is His Weakness

Since a mediator can take no action that binds the disputants, there is little or no harm he can do. His strength, derived in large part from the confidence of both sides, is his absence of strength: he cannot order the parties to settle on terms they oppose.

It is unwise for a mediator to make recommendations. He should hesitate even if both sides ask him to make recommendations. In most cases, his recommendations are more likely to please one side instead of both of the disputants. Once a mediator is openly committed to one side's position, he is likely to lose the confidence of the other side. In such circumstances, it will be difficult for him to continue to mediate.

Is it more important for a mediator or arbitrator to know how to mediate or arbitrate than it is for him to know the industry in which he is being asked to serve? The bankruptcy courts recommend as a key qualification that mediators possess knowledge of bankruptcy law. The

Internal Revenue Service places greater emphasis on their skills as a mediator.

It is more important that mediators know how to mediate than to know the industry in which they are serving. Obviously, knowing the industry can be a plus. But mediators can usually acquire the information they need to know faster than they can learn to mediate.

Disputants rarely think about third party assistance unless and until they reach an impasse in their talks, i.e., that point in the negotiations when the parties have made what they expressly or implicitly claim is their last, best offer and are still far apart on a settlement. Having asserted that they have nothing more to offer, they become understandably reluctant to propose mediation. If they have really made their final proposal, what is there to mediate?

But if they have merely claimed to have made their final offer, they need some way to get off the hook. For them to propose mediation would be self-defeating. They can be helped if a respected third party proposes mediation. In labor-management negotiations over the renewal of collective bargaining agreements, the Federal or State Mediation Agencies are required by law to offer their services at least 30 days before the expiration of the agreements. Their intervention relieves negotiators of the burden of proposing mediation after having said that they are at the end of the line on giving.

It is easier for the parties to accept mediation if proposed by a top public official or an eminent third party. They need only indicate that they are participating solely out of respect for the person proposing mediation. Such a response can help get mediation underway without impairing the integrity of their alleged "final" proposal.

It is not as difficult for disputants who have reached an impasse to propose arbitration. They can avoid implying that they might have more to give simply by saying that they are willing to have an arbitrator pass judgment on its fairness.

Sometimes a negotiator really means that he has made his final offer. The entrance of a mediator may then be troublesome for him. But the mediator may actually help him find a way out of the impasse. Regardless, a wise rule for negotiators is never to say never.

The pledge of the CPR Institute for Dispute Resolution, a private service provider with a distinguished roster of members, commits signers to consider ADR as an alternative to litigation. It is a useful device which helps avoid the appearance of weakness by a disputant who wishes to invoke mediation. If disputants informally indicate that they are not opposed to mediation but are reluctant to request that a mediator be appointed, a third party may solve the dilemma by proposing mediation and even suggesting who the mediator might be.

In disputes affecting the public, a government official may propose mediation—as President Johnson did in the 1964 railroad strike, Mayor Robert Wagner in the 114-day newspaper strike in New York City in 1963, and President Clinton in the months-long baseball strike in 1995. Cardinal O'Connor proposed mediation in a 1987 dispute between broadcast engineers and technicians and the NBC network, and it worked.

Participating in the Selection of Third Party Neutrals

Perhaps the greatest advantage of mediation or arbitration over litigation is the opportunity they provide the disputants to participate in the selection of the mediator and arbitrator to hear their dispute.

In litigation, the judge is selected in accordance with the court's system. In mediation and arbitration, both sides must agree either on the individual who is to be the mediator or arbitrator or on a method of selection.

The usual practice is for the parties to ask a qualified service-provider to submit a list of names. They can then strike the name of any person they question until they find a person both sides agree to accept. They can also ask for a second and even a third list or agree that the service-provider or a distinguished person make the choice.

Just as it is now permissible for lawyers to advertise, mediators and arbitrators can also hold themselves out as qualified practitioners in their particular field. But it is inadvisable for them to propose themselves in any particular dispute. They can, of course, have someone speak in their behalf.

Neutrals: Full or Part-time Professionals

In times past, mediators and arbitrators in labor management disputes rarely agreed to serve as negotiators for one side or the other. Lawyers tended to restrict themselves to representing either labor or management. As the relationship of labor and management has become less ideological and more pragmatic, lawyers now turn up representing companies in one case and unions in another.

In the beginning of my career, I served mainly as an arbitrator or mediator. Later, in specific cases, I represented one side or the other.

But I imposed on myself a firm rule: Having started in any relationship as a mediator or arbitrator, I would never move from serving as a neutral to either side in that relationship or vice versa.

At the time I represented the National Football League in negotiations with the Players Association, John Kiernan, the top sportswriter of the *New York Times,* mistakenly assumed that I was serving as a mediator and criticized me for favoring my clients. I had no difficulty straightening him out even though my actual role spoiled his story.

There was one *apparent* exception to my self-imposed restriction that was actually consistent with my rule against becoming an advocate in any situation in which I had served in a neutral capacity. I mention the circumstances of this apparent exception for the light it sheds on the variety of services a mediator can perform.

I became a mediator in New York's newspaper industry in 1963 and remained until 1978 in that capacity during a myriad of newspaper disputes. In August of that year, the pressmen's union struck the *New York Times,* the *New York Daily News* and the *New York Post* after the newspapers had unilaterally posted conditions reducing the number of men assigned to run each printing press.

The members of the 10 unions representing the various units of employees of the newspapers followed their time-honored practice of observing the pressmen's picket line. This brought the newspapers to a screeching halt.

I had not been invited by the parties to mediate the dispute and was not involved in the dispute.

But as the strike lingered on, George E. McDonald, president of the mailers union and the Allied Printing Trades Council, the umbrella organization of the City's newspaper unions, suggested that I mediate his union's open contract with the publishers in the hope that I might become involved in mediating the pressmen's strike. I told him I could not act as mediator in either dispute unless I was asked to do so by both sides.

I observed, however, that Rupert Murdoch, the publisher of the *Post,* whom the *Times* and the *Daily News* had appointed as their official spokesman, was repeatedly telling the members of the non-striking unions that they were being "ripped off" by the pressmen since they were supporting a union with demands in excess of their own goals and aspirations. I suggested that the Allied Printing Trades Council ask me to advise the unions on whether the pressmen were exploiting them. In effect, I would be acting as an impartial fact-finder in the conflict that Murdoch had promoted between and among the unions.

McDonald thought well of the idea, the Council duly voted to ask me to serve in that capacity and I agreed, since I would not be representing the unions but simply advising them on whether they were being taken advantage of by the pressmen's union. I also said that I would serve without compensation.

As I was serving as the unions' advisor, Murdoch withdrew from the negotiations, charging that I was conspiring with the *Times* and the *News* to put the the *Post* out of business. The federal mediator joined Murdoch's exit but the pressmen and the *Times* and the *News* remained in the negotiations and I assumed the role of mediator.

Shortly after he withdrew, Murdoch signed a "me-too" agreement with the unions, an agreement to accept whatever terms the *Times* and the *News* eventually negotiated. By signing the agreement, Murdoch was able to publish the *Post* while his competitors were on strike. He doubled the *Post*'s daily circulation and started up a Sunday edition which the Post desperately needed but had not been able to launch in the fierce competitive market it faced. Although the strike lasted quite a few days after Murdoch signed the "me-too agreement," it wasn't long enough for him to establish the Sunday edition as a viable publication and he was forced to fold the Sunday paper shortly after the other papers resumed publication.

A quote from Robert Browning's "The Lost Leader" was anonymously circulated among the remaining members of management and unions as well as the media. It read: "Just for a handful of silver he left us/Just for a riband to stick in his coat."

Former President Jimmy Carter, who has achieved some notable successes as an international mediator, has sometimes been criticized for appearing overly friendly with dictators and scoundrels on one side or the other of a dispute he is trying to mediate. But civility is an essential component of mediation in any field.

Kenneth W. Stein, a Middle East Fellow of the Carter Center who has observed Carter in negotiations on many occasions, said that the former President "purposely" divorced himself from any judgments about the person on the other side of the table. "He suspends what he might feel about that person as a person, or about the ideology that person articulates, or about that person's immediate past history. Most people say, 'How can you talk to these people who are dictators, who are brutal, who violate human rights—all those things that you don't like?' He has accepted in his mind that he has to divorce himself from what he thinks of the person in order to get the negotiations moving forward."

The approach is sound. As mediator, Carter can most effectively get the parties to agree with each other by treating them with respect and civility just as the UN Secretary-General must do with 185 member states. It would hardly serve a mediator's purpose to tell the spokespersons on either or both sides what he really thinks of them.

Meeting Privately with Each Side

It is unethical for an arbitrator to meet privately with either side without the express consent of the other side. A mediator is not subject to the same restriction since he has no power to decide the dispute. He is expected to meet separately with both sides. As discussed below, it is preferable for such meetings to follow an initial joint meeting in which the issues are clearly defined.

With the knowledge a mediator can gain through private conversations, he may be in a better position to encourage changes in the position of parties who might hesitate to advance proposals in face-to-face negotiations. The separate meetings can give the mediator a sense of the parties' concerns and of the perceived strength or weakness of their bargaining positions. They can also help him clarify the issues and assess the relevant facts. In multi-company or multi-union bargaining, private conversations with all parties can frequently help the mediator deal with differences within the company or union.

The negotiation of disputes in the private sector is a private matter. But if the dispute affects the public—as would a strike in a vital industry for example—the media obviously will be interested and cannot be kept away. The members of the fourth estate can be annoyingly persistent but their presence is usually accepted as unavoidable.

I was once conducting a secret meeting in a hotel suite I secured for the purpose. It was essential that the meeting be kept secret. We thought we had taken sufficient precautions, but as I opened the door at the meeting's end, there was the ever-present Tom Crane of the Associated Press. To this day, I do not know how he found out where we were meeting. Nor would Crane tell me.

The Issuance of Public Statements

As I point out in the next section, a mediator should discuss with the parties how, if at all, the media should be informed of the progress of the negotiations. If public statements are to be issued, he should try to persuade the parties to allow him to make them. Left to their own devices, the disputants will argue their cases in speaking to the media and most likely irritate their opponents.

To reassure the adversaries that they will not be embarrassed by any remarks he makes to the press, the mediator should agree to clear with both sides the substance of the statements he plans to make. The mediator can also suggest that if at any time either party believes that he must make a public statement, he inform the mediator in advance. That will give the mediator an opportunity to temper any provocative statements either side might be inclined to make.

If the parties are reluctant to refrain from speaking to the press, the mediator should at least insist on a blackout on press statements as the negotiation approaches the crunch, that point in the negotiations when no decision itself becomes a decision.

A Mediator's Compensation

A mediator who serves without compensation is often in a stronger position in shaping the course of the negotiations. If either or both sides fail to cooperate with him, he can simply announce that he will resign. The right of a mediator to resign is his strike weapon.

An arbitrator is in a different position. He does not have to persuade the parties to agree with each other. He has the power to make a final and binding decision regardless of how the participants behave. He can and usually does charge a daily fee, and has no reason not to be compensated for his services.

Even though I believe that a mediator can have greater leverage if he serves without compensation, it is unfair to expect anyone regularly engaged in mediation to serve without compensation. Besides, a mediator who enters a dispute that is likely to be long and intensive must be prepared to put all else aside for the duration of the negotiations. I have been in some disputes that lasted over, or just under, 100 days.

It has been my practice in such situations not to charge for my services as a mediator. It is not that I am in the business of resolving disputes as a hobby. I am always paid for my services as an arbitrator or negotiator. But I always believed that my ability to bring about a settlement as a mediator in major conflicts was significantly enhanced by my readiness to serve without payment. I saw my services as a contribution to a settlement.

FIVE PRINCIPAL ROLES
OF A MEDIATOR

THERE are five principal ways in which a mediator can assist the parties in reaching an agreement. They are as: 1) housekeeper of the proceedings; 2) ringmaster of the negotiations; 3) educator of the negotiators; 4) communicator between the disputants; and 5) innovator of creative approaches on substantive as well as procedural issues.

There are other things a mediator can do but the five include the main roles.

Role One: The Mediator as Housekeeper

The mediator should review the ground rules of his assignment. He should indicate that he will be the keeper of the records of the negotiations. He should also explain that his job is to help the parties agree with each other, that they have the right to make the final decision of resolution or disagreement and that he has no intention of telling them how the dispute should be resolved.

To reassure them that his role is simply to assist them in reaching an agreement, the mediator should make clear that he will make no recommendations unless asked to do so by both sides.

The mediator should suggest that the parties agree that, as the negotiations proceed and issues are necessarily discussed one at a time, any agreement on a particular issue shall not be deemed binding until all issues have been resolved. Such an understanding removes the negotiators' natural reluctance to advance concessions on separate issues before knowing what their opponent will agree to give them in exchange.

The mediator should also ask both sides to agree that they will not cite anything said by either side during mediation in any other forum. Such a stipulation will also help ease the give-and-take of negotiations.

Some states have adopted a rule specifically prohibiting disclosure of anything said during mediation.

If the dispute has attracted public attention, the mediator should discuss with the parties what statements, if any, should be released to the media and who should make them. It is best if both sides agree that the mediator should issue the statements with the understanding that he will clear them with the parties in advance.

If the mediator expects to be paid for his services, he should discuss his compensation at the outset of the talks.

Role Two: The Mediator as Ringmaster

I learned in a dispute I was mediating that the high-level engineers who coordinate the work of a team, as distinguished from those who work by themselves, are known as "ringmasters." The latter were referred to as "Einsteins."

The mediator chairs the meetings, determines how long they should last, when they should be recessed and whether and when separate meetings should be held. If he senses that an agreement is close at hand, he may keep the disputants in session and intensify their joint efforts to settle their dispute. If the discussions seem to be getting out of hand, he may call a short or extended recess.

The Mediator's Role in Defining the Issues in Dispute

A mediator most often enters a dispute after there has been bargaining for some time. Even if he has had prior dealings with the parties, he will probably have a lot to learn in a short time about the dispute at hand. He can serve the twin purposes of learning about the dispute and narrowing the differences between the parties if he sets out to have the issue or issues clearly defined.

Incidentally, as I moved from one industry to another, I found that each had a language of its own with which the disputants are so familiar they assume that the mediator knows what they are talking about. The mediator should not be reluctant to ask for definition of terms with which he is not familiar.

As I noted in Chapter One, I continue to be amazed by how frequently even the most sophisticated negotiators are sometimes unaware of the full dimensions of the issues and see them in an entirely different light than their opponents.

A mediator can be very helpful in defining the issues. The best way for him to proceed is by having both sides state their position to him in the presence of each other. If allowed to present their position separately, the negotiators will invariably state their claims in the light most favorable to their point of view. If they are in the same room, they will be subject to questioning by their opponents on the merits of their respective claims and inconsistencies or inaccuracies in their presentation. The mere presence of their opponent has a leveling influence on what they say. In the process, the mediator will garner information from the exchanges he would not get from separate meetings without pressing for answers that might impair his status as the impartial friend of both sides.

Identifying and Grouping Issues Under a Common Heading

An array of open and undefined issues need not be a nightmare. The mediator can introduce clarity by helping to define the issues and grouping related issues under a heading. If the mediator simply sums up the issues as neatly reassembled, he can create an air of accomplishment even though the basic issues remain unresolved.

The joint definition of the issues in dispute may take hours or even days. In one newspaper dispute, we took over two weeks to define and assess the issues. It was time well spent. The process of defining the issues helped mightily, not only to bring me up to speed, but also to bring the real goals of the disputants into sharp focus.

After identifying the issues in dispute, a mediator should ask both sides whether the resolution of those issues will end the dispute. If there is no affirmative reply, he should persist in making sure that all the issues are on the table. This prevents the introduction of new issues at the last moment of the negotiations, an occurrence that can seriously disrupt negotiations that have been brought under control.

During the course of listing and discussing the issues, I periodically tie up loose ends by saying, for example, "Well now, let me see if I understand you. In other words, you are seeking a concession that was turned down in the last negotiation," or some similar point that has not been fully developed.

I then ask the same or similar questions of the other side. An affirmative response from both parties means that the issues have been properly defined. This is the first step to a solution. It reduces the claims of both sides to their basic differences free of rancor or mistrust.

I then try to make a further grouping of the issues and to give each group a name tag. The identification, assessment and grouping of the issues should produce a complete picture. With each group representing an involved set of concepts, thought processes and positions, it becomes easier for the parties to discuss them. To make absolutely certain that the picture is complete, a mediator may find it useful to run through the issues once more, with as much additional grouping as possible.

This run-through will generally move fairly swiftly and may convey a sense of accomplishment and even relief. This is a good point at which to recess the negotiations to enable the parties to refresh and review their own positions.

I pursued the foregoing procedures upon entering the strike that shut down New York City's newspapers for 114 days in 1962/63. After a week of meetings, I had rearranged the innumerable issues in dispute and restated them in seven clearly defined groups of related issues. It looked as if the parties had actually made some progress. At that point, Jack Flynn, publisher of the *Daily News,* turned to me and politely said, "Congratulations, Mr. Kheel. You have reduced the issues in dispute to the insoluble ones." We became "Jack" and "Ted" at a later date.

The Order of Discussion in Disputes with Multiple Issues

It is virtually impossible to discuss more than one issue at a time. Nor are the parties expected to reach agreement on one issue after another. At most, they may agree tentatively on a particular issue, making their final commitment subject to agreement on all other issues. In what order, then, should the issues be discussed?

A mediator may sometimes seek to take up the minor issues first in the hope of creating an atmosphere of accomplishment by resolving one or more of them.

This may suit some negotiators who are reluctant to discuss the key issue or issues in dispute until the lesser ones have been resolved. Their concern is that a settlement on the main issue will make it difficult or impossible for them to get concessions on the minor issues. The other side, depending on the issues, may have exactly the opposite point of view.

The mediator should avoid any indication of a preference on the order in which the issues should be addressed. He should allow the decision to evolve through the discussions.

The Mechanics of Decision-Making

As ringmaster, the mediator should be concerned with how each party makes its decisions. It is helpful for him to know who is the ultimate decision-maker. But he should be careful not to go behind the backs of the negotiators that the parties have selected to speak for them at the bargaining table.

Just who is calling the shots is even more critical when an association of companies or unions is a participant in the negotiations. How do they arrive at their decisions? How are the decision-makers who are not present in the negotiations, and uninformed of the details and nuances, able to reach sound conclusions? Are they getting reports that reflect the spirit as well as the specifics of what is happening at the bargaining table?

The late Walter Thayer, a sophisticated negotiator who was president of the *New York Herald Tribune* during the 114-day strike and, as such, his newspaper's representative in the Publishers' Association of New York City, complained that "Trying to get a decision out of the Publishers' Association was like walking in a barrel of molasses."

The difficulty of decision-making, especially in multi-party negotiations, can be a continuing concern that a mediator must take into account.

It is frequently difficult in community disputes to establish the exact identity and authority of the complaining party—grievances against police and other law enforcement officials, landlords, hospitals and schools, for example. There may be several self-appointed "leaders" with different and conflicting aims and demands.

During the campus disturbances in the late 1960s, I was invited by the administration of Pennsylvania State University, then in the midst of a campus crisis typical of the times, to serve as mediator. The first question I faced was with whom should I meet? On the side of the University there were the President, the Dean and other administrators. But who spoke for the students? The self-appointed candidates included a group of vocal militants who were advancing attractive-sounding demands for far-reaching changes expressed in general terms. I met with a group of them but no one was designated as their principal spokesman. Nor were they clear on how their demands could be realized. We met again on several occasions and different individuals appeared each time.

At one point, I asked whether there were any formally designated student leaders and was told that there was an elected president and lesser officials of the student body. I then asked why I wasn't meeting with them. I was told that the elected leaders were not representative of their thinking. But how, I asked, could I tell what it was that the majority of the students wanted except by talking with their duly designated leaders? I never got a satisfactory answer. The Penn State controversy continued for months without a clear-cut resolution.

In a similar situation during the same period, I had occasion to meet with the black student protesters who had seized a building, Hamilton Hall, on the Columbia University campus. They were protesting the proposed construction of a gymnasium in a park area on Morningside Heights facing the adjacent Harlem community and had illegally seized and barricaded themselves in the building to enforce their protest.

My friend and colleague at the Metropolitan Applied Research Center, Dr. Kenneth B. Clark, suggested that the students ask me to meet with them to discuss resolving their dispute with the University. They agreed and I welcomed the opportunity. I climbed over the barricades in front of the building they were occupying and met with the students in a neatly arranged room with a desk in front, which their leader occupied. They were well mannered and in total agreement on what they wanted and why, but they had little awareness of what the University might be persuaded to agree to do.

Their leader, who presided at the meeting, asked me a pertinent question: what could I do to help them? I said I wasn't sure I could be of any help except to discuss with them what they could do to help themselves achieve their objective. I suggested that they should be clear about what it was they wanted to achieve and then focus on how they could get what they wanted. I pointed out that they would have to persuade the University to agree to give them what they wanted and that they should reflect on what they might do to get the University to agree with them. In the absence of an agreement, I observed, they were unlikely to achieve anything.

I was there for about an hour and the discussion was orderly and pointed. We spent most of the time on the mechanics of conflict resolution. I thought that they were getting to understand that conflict resolution through negotiation required the agreement of both sides and that, since they were the moving party, the key to a solution was getting the University to agree with them. I was pleased when they said that they wished to reflect on our discussion and would be in touch with me.

As I left the building, I was asked to meet with some 300 members of the faculty who had gathered in another building. I met with them for half an hour and heard almost 300 different views on how the crisis should be handled. I concluded that, for the purposes of conflict resolution, the faculty suffered from an abundance of independent thinking. It was clear that no consensus on what to do could emerge from discussions with them, and I left.

I then met with President Grayson Kirk and discussed with him a collateral question that invariably arises in disputes involving illegal actions: should amnesty be given to any participant in illegal actions? I agreed with President Kirk that students guilty of flagrant violations should not be allowed to return to classes. I added, however, that there remained unresolved who among the black students were guilty of the charges, and whether or not there were pardonable circumstances. I suggested that arbitration might be used in the event there remained any dispute issues.

President Kirk appeared mainly concerned about the reaction of his peers in universities throughout the country if he allowed any of the students participating in the takeover to return to class.

The students did try to meet with me that evening but were unable to reach me. As it turned out, President Kirk had undoubtedly decided before I met with him that there was no point in negotiating with the students. Later in the evening the police forcibly evicted the students from the building. On reflection, I concluded that it was highly unlikely that a negotiated settlement could have been achieved, even though, in my opinion, the students were ready to talk, and that is the first step to resolution.

Role Three: The Mediator as Educator

A mediator can be an educator even as he struggles to master the issues. He does this by encouraging each side to think of how to achieve their objectives while accommodating those of their opponents.

During the course of negotiations, the mediator will learn a lot about the dispute and the personal and political realities on both sides of the table. Very often a mediator will see the dispute in a light at variance with the way the parties see the dispute. It may be that he has missed points the disputants see because of their greater familiarity with the dispute. It is also possible for the mediator to have thoughts on approaches to a solution the parties do not possess. As I have said, the mediator should not tell the parties how he believes their dispute should be resolved. Instead he should help both sides understand the concerns of their opponents as they form their own conclusions on how the dispute should be settled. A mediator as educator can also help each side determine their priorities and clarify their positions.

A mediator should be careful not to damage the bargaining position of either side. As noted, he can make suggestions but should not make formal recommendations. He should be aware of the inherent myopia we all possess, necessarily seeing things from our own point of view. I repeat: a mediator can encourage the parties to see their opponents as they see themselves.

A company can easily convince itself that to give a wage increase is bad for the employees because it will drive up the cost of doing business, will make the company less competitive and will lead to a decrease in sales that will ultimately require it to lay off employees. Sincerely convinced, the company will express surprise that the union and employees see it otherwise.

What employees often believe is that the company is making lots of money, is seeking to make more by increasing profits at their expense and is hiding as much of the profits as it can through tricky accounting.

The mediator can perform a useful function by analyzing the arguments, preferably in separate discussions. He should never ask the company, "Why don't you offer more money?" or the union, "Why don't you settle for less?" Rather, his role is to lead them to reach such conclusions themselves.

It is perfectly permissible, and indeed wise, for a mediator to discuss the company's financial position with the union and to shed light on the company's profit and loss statement and balance sheet. The union officials can be asked whether they have looked at the financial reports the company has issued, about their understanding of the numbers, and whether they have thought about consulting an accountant.

The mediator can discuss with the company's officials whether the pressure for an increase in wages or benefits is the result of political factors within the union; whether it is related to a forthcoming union election; whether it stems from the union leadership, the rank-and-file, the cost-of-living or comparative wages in other plants; and the basis for their beliefs.

In whatever way he can, the mediator should try to stimulate discussions on the issues as they have been framed. Ironically, this might sometimes be more difficult with experienced negotiators who are fully familiar with the ploys and pleadings that each opponent is likely to undertake.

The Constraints of Experience

As mediator in a dispute in the New York Printing Industry, I tried unsuccessfully to get two seasoned negotiators, Elmer Brown, then Secretary and later President of the International Typographical Union, and Don Taylor, Executive Director of the Printing Employers Association, to address the sole remaining issue of wages after a very troublesome issue of union security had been settled.

We sat together for weeks of amiable conversation with neither negotiator ready to discuss the issue. In their considered judgment, it was not yet timely. We talked about the weather, baseball, politics and would lunch together and continue our talks later in the day. From time to time, I tried deftly to bring up the subject of wages but I was repeatedly rebuffed. In the minds of these experienced negotiators it was strategically unwise for either to say, "Let's talk about money, the issue we are trying to resolve."

When skilled negotiators are engaged in sophisticated negotiations, they can be sufficiently disciplined to speak out but say nothing until they conclude that the time for serious negotiation is at hand. They will also be sensitive to any changes in style or attitude and quick to interpret them. In between times, the negotiators are rarely adverse to pleasant small talk about everything but their unresolved dispute.

A skilled negotiator will also know how to talk without revealing any more than he is prepared to disclose. I have heard negotiators who keep saying that they want to bargain. "Come on," they'll say, "let's get down to business and settle this dispute." But if you listen carefully, you'll detect that they are far from ready to enter into serious discussions.

Under no circumstances should a mediator ask the question both sides are seeking to have the other answer: "What will you settle for?" It is a question no negotiator will answer until it is timely for him to do so.

A guest at a purely social gathering in the home of a publisher whose newspaper was on strike asked the publisher's wife what her husband would settle for if he could write his own ticket. She thought it was a brilliant question, assembled everyone at the party and asked her husband to answer it: "My dear wife," he responded, "you were 16 when I married you and your brains haven't grown since."

He turned around and then back again and quickly asked his wife: "Who is the spy that put you up to that question?" The party ended shortly thereafter. I have no knowledge of what the publisher and his wife said to each other after the incident, but I do know that their marriage survived until death did them part.

Cash or Credit: How They Are Shared

Beyond being paid for his services, if that is the arrangement, a mediator can be rewarded by the credit he gets for bringing about a settlement. But a mediator should also recognize that it is often wiser, indeed frequently necessary, to let the principal representatives of both sides get the credit.

The mediator should also bear in mind that negotiators tend to believe in the righteousness of their causes. But he can discreetly point out to the negotiators that the outcome of a negotiation is measured by what has been achieved regardless of who is right. Nor will it detract from the sweet smell of success if his opponent does not acknowledge defeat. As a wise old public relations specialist once told me, "Give credit if you want cash." This was his simple way of saying that it can sometimes help you to win what you want in negotiation by letting your opponent get the credit for the agreement.

The Ultimate Goal: A Win-Win Solution

A perfect outcome gives both sides a hundred percent of what they want. That is possible more times than most people realize. But it invariably calls for a reformulation of demands, usually based on a better understanding of what is required. It is sometimes referred to as a win-win solution.

By helping each side analyze its own requirements and those of its adversary, the mediator can help achieve such a solution.

Role Four: The Mediator as Communicator

A mediator is, above all, a communicator—an intermediary. Communicating through the mediator is often easier for a party to a dispute than communicating directly with the opposite side. Once an impasse has been reached, it may take the energy of a rocket launch to get the negotiations going again. Both sides are reluctant to take a forward step out of fear it will be viewed as a sign of weakness and a prelude to still another concession.

The mediator can help because often the parties will indicate to him a concession they will make if a corresponding modification is forthcoming from the other side.

When Dr. George W. Taylor and I were asked by President Johnson in 1964 to serve as mediators in the national railroad dispute that had been in contention for over five years, the nation's 523 railroads and the five operating unions were about as far apart as they were when their talks began. We were appointed as part of a 15-day truce that the President concluded after the unions struck one railroad and the carriers threatened to lock out the employees of all 523 railroads.

Many critical issues were at stake but a well advertised demand that the carriers had advanced was a major irritant. They insisted on a modification of the mileage rule set years earlier which entitled operators to be paid for a full day's work after a passenger train had traveled 100 miles and a freight train 150 miles. The carriers made the seemingly plausible argument that the mileage rates should be revised to take into account that the trains could travel far more in a day than they could when the mileage rule was adopted.

But the amount the operators were paid for a day's work had been adjusted over the years as pay scales went up. The existing formula was actually simply a method of calculating the amount of money the operators should receive for a day's work. The total payments the operators were receiving were roughly equivalent to those of employees whose pay scales were calculated in a different way.

At the outset of our mediation, James Reynolds, then Under Secretary of Labor, told me that James (Doc) Wolfe, the wily negotiator for the railroads, had to win some change in the mileage rates even if it was merely the addition of a mile. But any change, I told Reynolds, would require a wholesale revision of schedules and a new "pick of runs," a sacred right of railroad employees that enables them to choose in order of seniority where and when they work.

If the carriers held fast on the mileage rule, I added, I would not be able to avoid the belief that they did not want a settlement and were aiming, instead, to persuade Congress to impose compulsory arbitration to prevent a strike that would surely create a national emergency.

Shortly thereafter, Reynolds met privately with Wolfe and his associates and reported back to me that the railroads would drop this demand.

Since it is unwise to shock either side with unexpected developments they might instinctively reject, Taylor and I hesitated to tell the unions all at once that the carriers had agreed to drop their mileage demand. Instead, we asked the unions what they would give in return if we were able to persuade the carriers to drop that demand.

Their initial response, not surprisingly, was negative, probably because they weren't quite sure we could deliver the concession. When we said that we could not get the bargaining moving without some indication that the unions would make a meaningful response, the unions assured us that they would respond in kind.

To give validity to our claim that we were trying to get the carriers to drop their mileage demand, we allowed a suitable time to intervene before relaying the carriers' decision to the unions. Perhaps for strategic reasons, the unions were slow in responding. But their answer came and it was affirmative. I knew then there would be a settlement. It came within the 15 days the President had given us.

Transmitting Messages: The Care Required

A mediator faces great risks when he transmits messages. If he isn't careful, he may unintentionally convey a false signal from one side to the other that may alter the relative bargaining position of the parties and make the dispute more difficult to settle.

A mediator should take notes of what he is to transmit. To make sure he conveys the substance and tone of the communication accurately, he should review with the sender what he is going to say to the other side. A mediator should bear in mind that the negotiators will seek to get him to favor their proposals in communicating them to the other side. Returning from a meeting with one side, the mediator is surely going to be asked what the other side said. They will try to learn from him how the other side reacted to their communication.

Both sides are constantly looking for information that might reveal weaknesses in their opponents' bargaining position. In transmitting offers and counter-offers, a mediator must recognize that he may be conveying impressions that might add to or subtract from the bargaining position of either side. He should remember that the negotiators are attuned to nuances or words or suggestions that indicate a change, particularly a weakness, in their opponent's bargaining position.

Obviously, a mediator must respect the confidences of both sides. He should not only refrain from divulging any information he is specifically given in confidence, but not disclose anything that might alter the relative bargaining positions of the disputants even if he is not told that the information is confidential.

Role Five: The Mediator as Innovator

Having reached an impasse, the parties are generally reluctant to suggest new approaches to the issues in dispute lest their opponent see them as a sign of weakness. It is up to the mediator to get the dialogue going again and to find new ways of addressing and resolving the issues. Since he should avoid making recommendations unless specifically asked to do so by both sides, how can he be innovative?

There is a vast difference between making a "recommendation," which has a certain formality to it, and offering a "suggestion," which is less intrusive. A suggestion doesn't carry with it any implication that the mediator is telling the parties how the dispute should be settled. Even a suggestion should not be advanced in the presence of both sides. It can be offered to one side at a time.

A mediator can make a suggestion that is inoffensive simply by saying, "I had a thought. There may not be any merit to it, but what would you think of this kind of an approach?"

The response may be, "Forget it. It's out of the question" or "It may have merit, let's talk about it."

If the former, the mediator drops it and no one is hurt. If the latter, a discussion may be under way.

But if a mediator calls both sides together and says, "I have an idea. Why not do this, that, or the other thing?" he has taken a position that can be offensive to one side or the other.

Under no circumstances should a mediator raise questions in the presence of both sides that may be strategically embarrassing for either side. If he has any substantive suggestions to make that might be controversial, he should advance them in private conversations with each side. Even if asked to make recommendations, as I have previously observed, a mediator should reflect before saying yes. He should recognize that if one side accepts his recommendations and the other side rejects them, his ability to continue to mediate would be severely diminished.

There are circumstances in which the parties may want the mediator to make recommendations but are reluctant for strategic reasons to ask him to make them. One way to finesse that problem is to arrange for a respected observer who is not formally a party to the dispute to suggest that the mediator make recommendations.

If a mediator is satisfied that the parties are ready for him to make recommendations, he should deliver them directly to the disputants, and never release them to the media without the prior consent of both sides. A publicized statement on what the mediator recommends as a sound decision is a sure way to destroy any future role he might play in the negotiations.

Mutual Acceptance: The Aim of Recommendations

In making recommendations, the mediator's thought processes have to be along the lines of what is likely to be acceptable to both sides, not necessarily what is right from an equitable point of view.

The mediator succeeds only if both sides accept his recommendations. If one side rejects and the other accepts, the mediator and the dispute are in trouble. A better alternative is rejection by both sides.

This principle was dramatically illustrated in a dispute I was mediating between the *New York Times* and the Newspaper Guild, a white-collar union that includes reporters as well as clerical, service and administrative employees. One of the issues was the *Times*'s resistance to the Guild's demand for a union shop (the parties referred to the demand as the Guild Shop). The *Times* objected on the ground that if reporters were compelled to join the union, their objectivity and impartiality would be compromised.

As mediator, I had concluded that the reporters would not be biased as members of the union since the only significant obligation of membership under the Wagner Act as amended is the payment of dues. There is a political parallel. A member of one political party is required to continue to pay taxes even if the candidate he favored is defeated. The analogy is relevant since a union certified as the exclusive bargaining agent is obligated by law to represent all the employees in the bargaining unit regardless of whether they voted for the union or not.

I was asked by Mayor Wagner to report to him what I thought would be a fair resolution of the dispute and, with the consent of both sides, I agreed. In composing my recommendations, I concluded that the *Times* would reject the Guild shop, since it would be breaking ranks with other major publishers throughout the country, while the Guild would likely forego the Guild Shop if the settlement package included other benefits it was seeking for its members.

I decided, in consequence, to recommend against the Guild shop despite my expressed belief that it would not lead to bias in reporting of the news. As I anticipated, the Guild rejected my recommendations, which the Mayor had released to the public. The *Times* remained silent.

I heard this report on the radio while driving to the airport for a flight to Washington. I rushed to the nearest telephone and called the *Times*'s chief negotiator. "Your silence is deafening," I told him. "It implies that you might accept my recommendations." He seemed puzzled. "What's wrong with that?" he inquired. I replied by saying that if the *Times* accepted with the Guild rejecting, we'd never get the dispute settled. "But what can we say in rejecting recommendations we like?" he asked me.

I persisted. "Say anything as long as you reject my recommendations. Say that the report goes far beyond your expectations."

Ten minutes later, the *Times* was quoted on the air as saying that they had rejected my recommendations because they went far beyond what they expected. The next day the Mayor called both parties to City Hall where they accepted my recommendations.

Out of Conflict, Accord

The bargaining process itself, even at its most heated, can lead to creative solutions. The solutions can be simple or complex. In either case, if the mediator can keep the negotiations on track, accord can grow out of conflict.

During World War II, the United Automobile Workers threatened to strike an Olin Chemical Corporation plant, a major munitions maker. The Defense Department was, obviously, very disturbed. The union had just won a representation election but the company was challenging the results. There were many outstanding grievances and the union was insisting that the company and union seek jointly to resolve the grievances pending the outcome of the challenge.

Towards that end, the union proposed that the company recognize the union "on grievances." The company was adamantly opposed.

In the course of a dozen or so telephone calls, I suggested to the union, and then the company, that the War Labor Board recognize the union on grievances. The union agreed. The company was satisfied since it was not called upon to recognize the union. Both sides were glad to get the grievances addressed. The tripartite board of labor, management and public members voted unanimously to recognize the union on grievances, and the strike was averted.

In 1959, a 10-day strike by Local 1199 of the Retail Drug Employees Union against six voluntary non-profit hospitals in New York centered on the hospitals' refusal to recognize the union as bargaining agent for 3,000 non-professional hospital personnel. I suggested that the word "recognition," as used under the National Labor Relations Act, was irrelevant since non-profit hospitals were exempt from the NLRA at the time. I proposed that, without addressing the issue of recognition, the parties enter into a memorandum of understanding that would establish a formal grievance procedure. The parties agreed and the strike was ended.

As mediator in the 1962/63 newspaper strike that closed New York's newspapers, I received an urgent telephone call from the national president of the International Typographical Union, whose local affiliate was on strike. It is about time, he said, to get the strike settled. The members of the union nationally were contributing ten dollars a week in support of the members of the local union and he was under pressure from them to bring the strike to an end. We were able to arrange for Mayor Wagner, who was closely following the negotiations, to advance recommendations I drafted and cleared with the international union's president and the publishers.

Although acceptable to the leadership of the local union, the publishers and the president of the umbrella organization of all New York's unions, the recommendations were rejected principally by the members of the local union, who were receiving strike benefits almost equivalent to their regular salaries. A second ballot, held in secret on the city's voting machines, in which all of the members of the local union participated, including those who were contributing to the benefits the strikers were receiving, resulted in approval of the settlement.

In 1974, a creative solution with far-reaching consequences grew out of heated discussions in the newspaper negotiations in which I participated as the mediator. The issue was over the right of the publishers to use automated equipment, and the union's concern that many jobs would be lost as a result.

At one point in the meeting, Bertram Powers, the union's president, asked the publishers, "What will you give me for the green light?" By that he meant the elimination of all union restrictions on productivity that had accumulated over a century of collective bargaining. The answer came shortly thereafter: a guarantee that every typesetter on the

Front page picture of Mayor Robert F. Wagner, Daily
News *publisher Jack Flynn and Kheel celebrating the end
on March 20, 1963 of the strike that shut down New York's
12 newspapers for 114 days.*

payroll as of a given date would have a job for the rest of his life. The
reduction in force came about through attrition. As a result, membership in the union declined from about 6,000 in 1974 to 400 in 1999,
with productivity vastly increased.

A similar dispute arose at the turn of the century when an invention
that came to be known as the linotype machine (the name of the product of the principal company manufacturing them) replaced typesetting
by hand and became the way type was set until the computer revolution. A strike at the *New York Sun* that lasted three years was finally
resolved with an agreement that allowed the publisher to use the linotype machines. In exchange, the employees were granted an eight-hour
work day.

In the 1974 dispute, Powers was insistent on a reduction in hours.
The publishers took the position that if they reduced hours for the

typographers, they would have to reduce hours for the members of the other nine unions. The dispute posed the problem of "me-tooism" which is present in many, if not all, multi-union or multi-company negotiations. It is a problem the New York publishers continuously faced with the ten unions representing the ten crafts of the newspaper industry and the unions faced in dealing with more than one competing newspaper.

On the reduction in hours, the publishers were adamant. The concession would spread immediately to the other unions. Finally, they proposed one week of additional vacation as part of the agreement on automation, a concession that would not break new ground. The union rejected the offer. But the parties had agreed upon an 11-year contract of which two years had already elapsed with nine to go. I suggested a reformulation of the publisher's offer under which the typesetters would be given a sabbatical of nine weeks once during the life of the contract. Both sides accepted my suggestion.

Negotiations in New York City in 1968 between the city-owned transit system and its workers over pension rights provided another opportunity for an innovative approach. The union demanded that employees be given the right to retire with a pension after 20 years of service, a provision already won by the sanitation workers. A union is always under pressure to obtain benefits for its members won by another group, especially one with the same employer.

The Transit Authority, already hard-pressed to recruit and retain skilled workers, was fearful that retirement after 20 years of service without reference to age, would open up the possibility of a worker taking his pension too early. Such a reduction would take many skilled workers, those most difficult to replace, out of service. That was of greater concern to the Transit Authority than the cost of the pension. This issue dominated the dispute and appeared to be an insurmountable obstacle.

The board of mediators, of which I was a member, together with Vincent McDonnell, chairman of the New York State Board of Mediation, and Joseph E. O'Grady, former chairman of the Transit Authority and a man held in high esteem by the union and the workers, undertook to reformulate the issue.

The retirement age for transit workers was 55 and it was difficult to object to the union's argument that a transit worker retiring at that age with 20 years' service, a right already won, was entitled to as large a pension as a sanitation worker. His cost of living in retirement was the same as a sanitation worker even if, as the sanitation workers had argued, their job entailed greater physical risks and injuries.

We then pointed out to the union that if the workers received assurance of the sanitation formula for benefits, the issue would be reduced to the question of whether a transit worker should be able to retire with a pension at age 40 if he had begun service when he was 20 years old. There was no social justification for such a contention and the union would have had a difficult time mobilizing a strike on that issue.

The union was forced to acknowledge that the argument for such early retirement was weak, especially since the probability was that retirees would not stop work but enter a new profession. Why should they not remain with the Transit Authority, especially since they would continue to accumulate pension credits? Nevertheless, the example of the sanitation workers continued to trouble the competitive sense of the transit workers.

The union first persisted in proposing an age minimum of 45 but finally agreed to retirement at age 50 after we reviewed the statistics showing that only a few people would be affected if the retirement age were 50.

For the Transit Authority, the reduction did not appear as critical since it was highly unlikely that a man would seek a new career at 50. He would have no expectation of any pension benefits on the new job and could continue to improve his pension rights by remaining with the Transit Authority.

In some cases a similar attempt to reduce critical issues to their basic differences is less successful, but the mediator is always looking for ways to take disputes out of the level of principle and into the realm of practicality. In labor relations, as in other human affairs, parties are willing to assume great risks on matters of principle but are also often ready to be less rigid if the issue can be reduced simply to a difference in money.

I always like to put a price tag on each issue after they have been defined. A mediator has an advantage if he can narrow the strike issue to a few people or a few dollars. At the same time it is essential that he as well as the parties understand who will be affected, and how the union and employer are likely to react.

Older workers with considerable seniority may be entitled to and receive more attention from the union and employer than new employees. The steps on the pay scale and the differentials between steps as well as the maximum salary may be more important than the starting rate. At the same time, the employer may be concerned about his ability to attract new employees and he may be eager to have the increase come at the start of employment.

Timing and Patience: A Mediator's Indispensable Tools

Patience is a mediator's indispensable tool. The clock is his pilot. It tells him when he should change direction. There are times for decision-making, and times when nothing can be accomplished. It is difficult to get the parties to make changes before the crunch—that point in a negotiation when no decision becomes a decision. In such circumstances, it is not unusual for a mediator to keep the parties in session even if it means going around the clock. The early morning hours, when fatigue sets in can be the right time to resolve simple issues that have been thoroughly explored. On the other hand, it may be exactly the wrong time if complex issues are at stake.

Collective bargaining, like all forms of negotiation, entails decision-making. Decisions are often postponed as untimely. They are often avoided out of fear of making the wrong decision. But a time inevitably comes when the failure to decide becomes a decision because something else is bound to happen. That time frequently arrives in collective bargaining when a failure to say yes or no leads the other side to take actions that alter the status quo. A strike or lockout is a classic example.

Keeping an Eye on the Clock

The parties will likely be aware of an approaching crunch. But they will be inclined to appear unconcerned about its arrival. The mediator should keep a close eye on the clock. He will decide, as the hour of greatest pressure on both sides draws near, when the parties should meet or recess and when to keep them in session.

If a deadline passes without a settlement and a strike begins, there is an inevitable hardening of positions. Parties may be exhausted and settle into a mood of siege. There may also be a desire to find out the extent to which the other side is hurting before resuming serious deliberations.

A mediator's efforts, no matter how strenuous, are likely to be unavailing immediately after a strike begins. But a mediator has the best chance of bringing a settlement about at the moment of crunch and he should be on the lookout for deadlines that can help precipitate decision-making.

During the newspaper dispute of 1965, I tried to use the forthcoming visit of Pope Paul to New York as a crunch date in a dispute in which the parties seemed disinclined to come to grips with the issues before them. I stressed how important it was for all concerned to have the city's newspapers in circulation during this historic event. I thought that would stimulate realistic negotiations to reach a settlement before the date of the Pope's arrival. But I underestimated the importance of the issues to the newspapers as well as the unions. The Pope's visit began with the newspapers closed and they remained closed for many days after his departure. The internal pressures on both sides eventually brought the dispute to an end.

The threat of a strike or the unilateral imposition of new terms of employment can be an effective inducement for decision-making. For that reason, it is generally inadvisable for a mediator to talk about postponing the strike deadline since it is really the threat of a disruption that instills the bargaining with a sense of urgency to reach an agreement. As the moment of decision approaches, every advantage has been drawn from the deadline. If it appears that an accord is near, it is possible to suggest a short postponement.

In the 1967 transit negotiations in New York the contract expired at 5 AM on January 1, 1968. Just before the deadline the union postponed the strike for three hours without announcing this change. The tension at the bargaining table was preserved for a few more minutes and the urge to reach agreement was intense. When the postponement was announced, the pressure naturally subsided and very little was accomplished. Then, with a new deadline approaching, there was a renewed sense of urgency at the bargaining table, and this pressure was effective in leading the parties to an agreement.

Decision-Making in Group Negotiations

The representatives at the bargaining table in group negotiations face varying problems of decision-making. The mediator can be of assistance to both sides. But he must understand the problems each side faces.

The problems of group leadership and group relations in labor-management contests, for example, are much different on the union's side than those the employer faces. The employer's representatives rarely have to confer with their principals, the stockholders. In employer associations, however, differences may sometimes surface. The union's principals are the rank and file. They are only consulted after an agreement has been reached at the bargaining table and, in most cases, is made subject to rank and file approval.

The mediator should seek, as unobtrusively as possible, to find out about these differences without ever intruding in the internal affairs of either side. The mediator must also be mindful of internal frictions within the negotiating committees. Such divisions may not be evident on the surface, but they can be impediments to a satisfactory resolution of the dispute.

In some wage disputes, the employer may offer a gross sum, leaving it to the union, with or without the mediator's assistance, to work out the allocation. In so doing, the mediator must understand the problems faced by the union leadership in dealing with different factions in the union. It is at times wise (but at other times improvident) to leave such questions exclusively to union leadership. In many situations the mediator may have to work out an allocation formula with the employer's participation.

Agreements Requiring Group Approval

Often agreements reached in group negotiations must be submitted to a membership for approval. This happens frequently in labor-management negotiations. The union leaders then face a difficult problem in communication since their members have not been present during the bargaining sessions. They must be persuaded that they were effectively represented and their interests well served.

A negotiator who enters into an agreement at the bargaining table that is subject to the approval of the members has a moral obligation to urge adoption of the agreement and to make certain that the terms are properly considered by the principals who were not at the bargaining table. If a leader is insecure and merely acts as a messenger, the likelihood of rejection is vastly increased.

Reporting to the rank-and-file the results of a tentative agreement may require the cooperation of both sides and here the mediator can play an important part. The negotiators in the settlements reached in 1998 between the Protestants and Catholics in Ireland and the Palestinians and Israelis in the Middle East faced severe problems in persuading their principals that the agreements they reached should be ratified.

A Brief Summation

The mediator's job is to assist the parties in reaching the agreement they might have reached if, for one reason or another, an impasse had not developed in their negotiations. He is there to help the parties agree with each other; he is not there to propose the solution he thinks they should reach. It is important that he not distort the bargaining process to produce a result inconsistent with the outcome the parties would likely reach by themselves.

TEN COMMANDMENTS FOR MEDIATORS

    I. Emphasize at the outset the importance of clearly defining the issues in dispute and gathering and assessing the relevant facts.

   II. Take control of the "housekeeping" aspects of the dispute such as where and when the meetings should be held, how long they should last and whether and when public statements should be made to the media.

  III. Remember, your goal is to get the disputants to agree with each other; it is not to influence them to agree with your views on the merits of their respective claims.

  IV. Avoid any statements or actions that will prejudice the bargaining position of either side.

   V. Make no formal recommendations for settlement unless both sides specifically ask you to do so and, if requested, bear in mind that your ability to continue mediating may be prejudiced if one side accepts your recommendations and the other side rejects them.

  VI. You may offer suggestions for discussion purposes, separately or to both parties, but not as a recommended solution.

 VII. Convey accurately any messages or proposals you are asked to relay to the other side.

VIII. Respect any confidences you are given by either side.

  IX. Never go around the individuals designated by each side as their spokespersons; as the Bible says, "Accuse not a servant to his master."

   X. Bear in mind at all times that you are the friend of contesting adversaries. Give them no reason to share you as an enemy.

CHAPTER SIX

THE STRUCTURE OF VOLUNTARY ARBITRATION

THOUGH arbitration is voluntary, it is closely related to litigation. Both are forms of adjudication (which the dictionary defines as a "judicial decision") since, in both procedures, a third party makes the final decision.

An arbitrator is given the power by agreement of the disputants; our court system vests a judge or jury with the power to make the final decision. Arbitration is less formal than court proceedings, but the decision of the arbitrator is final and binding.

Rights and Interest Arbitrations

As previously noted, there are two main types of disputes that can be resolved through voluntary arbitration: those involving claims that a law or contract has been violated and those arising out of interest claims the courts can't resolve, such as the price a seller should receive or a buyer pay.

Rights arbitrations are usually conducted pursuant to an agreement of the parties to resolve future disputes over the meaning and application of the terms of the agreement. Such agreement usually provides that the arbitrator has no power to add to, or subtract from, the terms of the agreement.

Most international contracts between parties from different countries contain provisions for the arbitration of rights disputes, and virtually all collective bargaining agreements have similar provisions.

In three precedent-making decisions generally referred to as the Steelworkers Trilogy, the United States Supreme Court affirmed the arbitration of grievances as the preferred procedure for resolution of workplace disputes. The courts have also ruled that, despite the ban on injunctions in labor disputes, injunctions against strikes or lockouts can be issued if the agreement between the company and union provides for the arbitration of disputes arising under the agreement. This accounts for the stability of the labor-management relationship during the term of the collective bargaining agreement.

In interest disputes, the parties generally enter into an agreement to submit the dispute to arbitration; the agreement spells out the criteria the arbitrator must use in deciding the dispute.

For understandable reasons, far more rights than interest disputes are submitted to arbitration. In rights arbitration, the arbitrator is simply called upon to interpret and apply to the dispute before him the terms of agreement the parties have already negotiated. In interest arbitrations, the parties are contesting the terms of an agreement they have not been able to negotiate. In agreeing to arbitration of such terms, the parties must first agree on the criteria the arbitrator is to apply in making his decision. If they can get that far, they usually can reach an agreement on the terms in dispute.

In labor-management disputes over the terms of collective bargaining agreements, the issues can concern such fundamental matters as compensation, job security, productivity, downsizing, pensions and health care. Both sides are understandably reluctant to have a third party decide such issues. Most often, they would rather risk a strike or lockout than cede control to an outsider.

A Dramatic Rejection of an Interest Arbitration Proposal

On February 21, 1963, President Kennedy blasted Bertram Powers, the leader of the strike that shut down the *New York Times* and nine other New York City newspapers for 114 days beginning on December 6, 1962. He also proposed that the contractual issues in dispute be submitted to arbitration. Powers politely rejected the proposal, simply saying that the President was misinformed. As the mediator, I knew that Powers was adamantly opposed to interest arbitration and that the publishers were equally reluctant to have the critical issues at stake decided by a third party. But they would likely have agreed to arbitration if Powers had accepted.

What I didn't know, until I received a telephone call from President Kennedy, was that Philip Graham, the publisher of *Newsweek* and the *Washington Post,* had told the President that he was wrong about Powers and that it was the publishers who were to blame for the strike. Kennedy was disturbed and immediately sought advice from Justice Arthur J. Goldberg, who had represented labor unions in collective bargaining until Kennedy first appointed him Secretary of Labor and then named him to fill a vacancy on the Supreme Court. Goldberg suggested that the President call me.

I was having dinner at the St. Regis Hotel in New York City on Sunday evening, February 24, 1963, and learned from one of my children when I called my home for telephone messages that the President was trying to reach me from the Kennedy compound in Palm Beach, Florida. I called the operator in Palm Beach from a pay booth in the hotel and was quickly connected with the President, whom I had met once before in a crowded room. Kennedy promptly told me about the call he had received from Graham and that he was troubled by it. Phil, he said, had been very helpful to him in Los Angeles at the Democratic convention that nominated Kennedy and Johnson. He added, however, that Graham had not been well and that he was uncertain about what Graham had told him about Powers and the publishers. The President asked me to contact Graham, who was at the Carlyle Hotel in New York, and to call him back after I had spoken to Graham.

I met with Graham for several hours in his suite at the Carlyle and learned from him that *Time* magazine, *Newsweek*'s chief competitor, was carrying a major story about the newspaper strike with Powers on the cover, and that he had met with Powers in New York on Saturday to get first-hand information about the demands he was making. After Powers gave him a run-down on his demands, which were extreme by any standard, Graham quickly told him they were reasonable and called the President in Powers' presence to tell him that he made a mistake in criticizing Powers instead of the publishers. It was that call that led the President to get in touch with me.

Graham then asked me if I wanted to settle the strike. I told him that I had been trying for over 80 days to get it settled. "Here's the way you can end the strike," he replied. "Get Mayor Wagner to name me chairman of a board of arbitration. I don't care who else he appoints. We'll make a decision that will end the dispute."

I said that Powers would not agree to arbitration and that the publishers were also opposed. "Do you want Powers to agree?" he asked me. "Of course I do," I replied. "With Kennedy's insistence, the publishers would probably go along."

Graham then went into the adjourning room of his suite and called Powers on the telephone. He returned a while later to say that Powers would not agree to arbitration. He then asked me to persuade the

Mayor to name him to mediate the dispute. I politely declined to arrange to be replaced.

I later learned from Powers that Graham gave Powers the terms of an award he would make if he was named chairman of a board of arbitration. His proposed award would have given Powers virtually everything he was asking of the publishers. Consistent with his position on the arbitration of interest disputes, Powers declined to agree to the arbitration of his demands even though Graham had told him what the award would contain. Powers also told me he assumed there was something wrong with Graham.

And indeed there was. Graham, it was later disclosed, was suffering from a mental disorder that led to his suicide a few months thereafter. I have recounted this sad episode simply to emphasis the extent to which both labor and management oppose interest arbitrations of their differences.

As noted, arbitration can be compulsory if imposed by legislation. It is an extreme measure that Congress and State legislatures are likely to enact only in cases threatening national or local health or safety.

Congress has imposed arbitration in a number of railroad labor disputes and some states require unresolved disputes involving policemen and firemen to be arbitrated. At the time the Postal Service was made an independent public corporation, Congress passed legislation mandating arbitration of unsettled interest disputes between the Service and the unions of its employees.

The postal legislation specified that disputes over the terms of collective bargaining agreements should be decided by a tripartite board consisting of one member appointed by the Post Office, another by the Postal Union and the third selected by the party-appointed arbitrators.

I served as the arbitrator appointed by the American Postal Workers Union in two major postal arbitrations over interest claims the parties were unable to resolve. We reached satisfactory conclusions in both disputes. As I observed in Chapter Two, arbitration by boards composed of party-appointed arbitrators in addition to a neutral arbitrator work best in interest disputes where compromise is possible.

If there is no viable alternative to a strike or lockout except compulsory arbitration, a board of party-appointed arbitrators with a neutral chairman is the way to proceed. But negotiation is far and away the best approach for resolving interest disputes.

The Enforceability of Arbitration Awards

In an unusual dispute between the Amateur Athletic Union and the National Collegiate Athletic Association over the sanctioning (approval) of track meets, the United States Senate adopted a resolution calling on these arch enemies to submit their differences to arbitration before a board that Vice President Humphrey was empowered to name. The resolution was designed to eliminate potential problems in the selection of U.S. athletes in track and field events for the 1968 Olympic Games in Mexico City.

The Vice President asked me to serve as chairman and named as my fellow members Harvard Professor Archibald Cox, the former Solicitor General and later Watergate Special Prosecutor; Ralph Metcalf, the 1932 and 1936 Olympic Track Superstar and then a Chicago Alderman; General David Shoup, retired Commandant of the U.S. Marine Corps; and Thomas Vail, publisher of the *Cleveland Plain Dealer*.

Conflicts between the AAU and NCAA threatening U.S. participation in the 1964 Olympics had arisen in the early 1960s. At that time, President Kennedy requested General Douglas MacArthur to resolve them, and not long before his death, the General arranged a truce, or moratorium, which was satisfactory as a temporary expedient for the 1964 games. But the truce did not resolve the dispute.

The conflict arose again and threatened U.S. participation in the 1968 Olympics. For reasons I never discovered, the dispute was referred to the Senate's Interstate Commerce Committee, which prepared the resolution that led to our appointment.

The dispute turned out to be far less serious than the high level of attention it was receiving. During the course of extensive hearings, our board found out that at the root of the conflict was the insatiable appetite of the bureaucracies of the two organizations over who would get most of the money and perquisites that the televising of sporting events was beginning to generate. The AAU had a leg up simply because it had been controlling qualifications for participation in the Olympics for many years and the NCAA offered no persuasive reason to change the established system.

We issued a unanimous award and the Senate Interstate Commerce Committee backed us up. The AAU accepted, but the NCAA and its satellite organization, the United States Track and Field Federation, rejected. I wrote a letter advising the 600 college and university presidents that I was "shocked and horrified" by the rejection of our award by their representatives. In a remark the *New York Times* selected as the quote of the day, I said, "These people [meaning both sides] make the Teamsters look like undernourished doves."

Unlike arbitrations imposed by legislation enacted by both houses of Congress and signed by the President, the Senate Resolution by itself did not have the force of law. But the parties had agreed to participate and they might have been deemed to have entered into a binding agreement to arbitrate. I stated publicly that they were morally, if not legally, bound to comply with our award. But there were lingering doubts about the award's enforceability.

The AAU appeared reluctant to move in the courts to enforce the award and the NCAA had no incentive to go to court. But this monumental clash, which was basically over fees and perquisites for bureaucrats, and which neither General MacArthur nor our board could solve, somehow disappeared and the Olympics moved on with the full participation of our athletes.

The Selection Process: An Advantage of Arbitration Over Litigation

As I have mentioned, one of the great advantages of arbitration over litigation in the private sector is the opportunity it offers the disputants to take part in the selection of the arbitrator.

A number of service providers offer disputants information about individual arbitrators. An organization known as LRP Publications currently advertises that it provides Instant Computer Arbitration Search on some 68,000 published arbitration awards and that the decisions are listed by arbitrator, by company, by subject and by union. They also provide personal information about the arbitrator and the extent of his experience.

Of course, each side must get the consent of the other not only on the submission of their dispute to arbitration, but on the selection process as well. The selection process can become a critical issue in the negotiation over arbitration.

In exercising their veto rights, the disputants should consider the qualifications of proposed candidates in light of the issue or issues at hand. Lawyers make good arbitrators on issues involving the interpretation and application of the terms of an agreement. I have found academics to be particularly sensitive on productivity issues. They favor efficiency. They are also mindful of the impact of wage increases on inflation. They tend to support demands for union or employee security.

There is another significant advantage of arbitration over litigation: it allows the parties to fashion their own forum of dispute resolution. In litigation, the rules of the court govern the conduct of the proceeding. In negotiating with each other, the disputants can agree on when and where the arbitration should take place, the extent to which discovery should be allowed and the criteria the arbitrator should observe in making his decision. But to enjoy these advantages, the parties must reach agreement with each other, and that is not always an easy matter.

An Unusual Contractual Provision on the Selection of Arbitrators

I represented Lester Osterman, a producer of Broadway plays, in a dispute with comedienne Carol Burnett. The issue concerned whether she had violated her contract to remain for the run of the play as the star of "Fade In–Fade Out," a musical play that opened to approving notices on February 15, 1964.

In 25 weeks Ms. Burnett missed 58 performances, allegedly as a result of back and neck ailments. Invariably, when she failed to appear, most of the audience asked for a refund. When she withdrew, the producer was forced to close the show. He sustained a loss of $500,000.

We believed that Ms. Burnett was feigning her injuries to get out of the show for personal reasons and we moved under the collective bargaining agreement to compel her to honor her contract and return to the show.

The collective bargaining agreement contained an unusual provision. It vested in Actors Equity, the union that represented Ms. Burnett, the power to name a five-member board of arbitration. We had no choice but to comply with the agreement and went to trial before a board of five actors named by the actors union.

Surprisingly, the board appeared to side with us. As actors, they seemed to subscribe to the theater's credo that "the show must go on." They were also faced with evidence placing Ms. Burnett's claim of injuries in severe doubt. In the middle of the hearing, Ms. Burnett charged us with impugning her reputation, threw in the towel and agreed to return to the show.

At considerable cost, the show was remounted and reopened to responsive audiences. Soon after, Ms. Burnett disclosed that she was pregnant and entered a hospital allegedly out of fear she might have a miscarriage. The show closed immediately. It remained closed as her stay in the hospital continued. It was finally closed permanently. Shortly thereafter, her representatives announced that she had a miscarriage. We were distressed and disturbed but remained impressed with the integrity of the board of arbitrators that the union had appointed.

Permanent Versus Ad Hoc Arbitrators

In many situations, particularly in collective bargaining agreements and ongoing commercial contracts, the parties may designate a permanent arbitrator to whom they can readily turn for resolution of disputes over the meaning or application of the terms of the agreement. With knowledge of the industry and the parties, a permanent arbitrator can help stabilize the relationship. He is also handy to have around in situations where there are likely to be many disputes including some that require immediate attention.

While serving as permanent arbitrator in the New York City transit industry, I would often receive a call advising me that if an arbitration was not conducted within the next hour or two, there might be a work stoppage. I would immediately arrange a hearing to suit the time constraints of the disputants. I even conducted several arbitrations on the telephone.

An arbitrator in a rights dispute is obligated to confine himself strictly to the terms of the agreement that he is called upon to interpret and apply. If the terms are ambiguous, he will be asked to determine what the parties had in mind when they wrote the provision in question. He functions in this respect as a judge would in similar circumstances.

But there are also terms on which there may be a range of possible solutions. Take, for example, a traditional provision in a collective bargaining agreement on violations that might lead to an employee's discharge. A standard provision would state that employees shall not be discharged except for just cause or, affirmatively, that employees can be discharged only for just cause. But what is just cause? It can vary with the circumstances.

In exercising his judgment on such issues, the arbitrator should take into account that the parties have an ongoing relationship and will have to continue to work together after his decision is made. The decision should come within the range of those the parties might expect in the circumstances. He should look to what arbitrators have done in similar cases. If an employee is discharged for absenteeism, the arbitrator should consider whether he has missed several or many assignments and whether there are any other extenuating circumstances. A certificate from a reputable physician might be relevant.

Adhering to the Rule

The importance of adhering to the precise issue presented to the arbitrator cannot be overestimated. The arbitrator should avoid *obiter dictum,* i.e., any remarks irrelevant to the decision. His decision should be confined to the case before him.

I was called upon to arbitrate an issue that was a critical part of a dispute that threatened the Metropolitan Opera's entire 1961–62 season. The issue involved a contract renewal dispute between Local 802 of the American Federation of Musicians and the Metropolitan Opera Association.

At President Kennedy's request, Secretary of Labor Arthur J. Goldberg, a former general counsel of the AFL-CIO, entered the dispute and was handed a full plate of more than 100 issues for decision. Among them were the amount of the weekly wage, the length of the contract, day rehearsal and pre-season rehearsal rates, over-night per diem allowances and grievance procedures—all standard fare for conventional labor-management bargaining.

Secretary Goldberg used his arbitration award of December 14, 1961 to resolve most of the issues at stake and also to call for government subsidies to all the performing arts—later to be achieved through the National Endowment for the Arts. This proposal earned Goldberg national attention, including a front-page story in the *New York Times.*

But there was one issue Goldberg did not decide and it was the bitterest one in the dispute. It had to do with the Metropolitan's refusal to rehire Lester Salomon, for 20 years a Met French horn player and an active member of the union's committee. The Met contended that Salomon had "lost his lip and was no longer capable of performing adequately." Salomon was convinced that he was turned down because of his union activities. Goldberg named me to arbitrate that dispute and the parties agreed.

I was immediately asked by the media about my qualifications to pass on Salomon's continued ability to play the French horn. I could only tell them that I was banned from singing at my graduation from grade school because the sounds I uttered were not in harmony with the music as written.

But the precise issue I was asked to decide was not Salomon's continued ability to play the French horn. It was whether he was discharged because of his union activities. I was able to pass on that issue and concluded that he was not discharged for that reason. I made no determination of Salomon's ability to play the French horn and said nothing about it.

The award was greeted with long and loud boos from the union's side. It led the *New York Herald Tribune*'s editorial department to observe that, "[W]e imagine Mr. Kheel and probably Mr. Goldberg as well would be glad to confine their further operatic adventures to a comfortable seat in the parterre." It was the last Metropolitan Opera dispute I handled. But I had adhered to the requirements of the collective bargaining agreement.

Rex Harrison's Replacement in "My Fair Lady"

As "My Fair Lady" was nearing the end of its run with Rex Harrison in the lead, I was asked to arbitrate whether he should be replaced by Edward Mulhare, another Englishman, as the producers sought, or by an American as Actors Equity, the union of actors in Broadway shows, wanted. Actors Equity was motivated in large part by the insistence of its British counterpart that Englishmen be played by actors from their country.

I was hardly qualified to decide who was the best actor to play the role of Professor Henry Higgins. But I knew that the test should not be the actor's country of origin. I ruled that Mulhare should get the role and did not have second thoughts about my decision when I later concluded, on seeing Mulhare in the show, that Harrison was irreplaceable.

McCarthy vs. McCarthy, McCarthy and McCarthy

Though frequently as intense as the Salomon case, not all grievance arbitrations are as grave.

An example in point is the case of Dennis McCarthy, bus operator for a New York bus company then privately owned, versus Joseph J. McCarthy, his immediate superior, Joseph T. McCarthy, vice president of the company and John E. McCarthy, president. It grew out of D.

McCarthy's claim for reimbursement for the day's work he lost on December 31, 1952 when he was suspended for refusing to repay $12.90 he owed the company. He did not deny he owed the money but claimed that, for reasons never disclosed, the company was out to get him.

In an extensive presentation that dwelled on how convinced he was of his own honesty, D. McCarthy refused to cut his presentation short despite the complaint of a company representative that he was wasting everybody's time with irrelevancies. Insisting that everything he was saying was exactly to the point, D. McCarthy obligingly offered to and did thereafter talk faster.

The dispute first arose when D. McCarthy failed to report on the day card that drivers fill out at the end of their run that he had worked to the end of his run. Also omitted were the readings on his fare box. Without that information, the payroll department deducted $6.45 from his next paycheck, the amount it estimated as due. D. McCarthy immediately complained and was told to fill out the form and that he would be paid the full amount.

But the form he was given did not include the fare box readings. They were no longer available. As a man of honorable principles, as he modestly admitted, D. McCarthy would not sign the form without the readings even though his supervisor told him to put down any numbers whose difference equaled the amount of his receipts for the day in question. Instead, he sent the day card to the union with no explanation. It languished in the union's office, since the officials did not know why it had been sent.

When his next pay check did not include the $6.45, D. McCarthy, adhering to his principles, resorted to self help: as he testified, he "dipped" into the fares he collected that day by deducting $6.45 from them. The company responded by deducting $6.45 from his next paycheck and again pleaded with him to fill out the day card.

As a self-described man of honor, D. McCarthy continued to refuse to enter fictitious numbers on his day card. Instead he again deducted $6.45 from his next day's receipts. Once again, the company responded by deducting $6.45 from his next paycheck.

Showing admirable restraint, D. McCarthy withheld any retaliatory measures until the last payday of the year. Anticipating that the company would expect that he would again deduct $6.45 from the company's receipts, D. McCarthy retaliated in advance by withdrawing $12.90 from the receipts.

Having apparently concluded by this time that it would be less time consuming and expensive in the long run if it accepted D. McCarthy's method of accounting and concentrated full time on running the buses, the company did not deduct anything from his pay check. As a result, D. McCarthy had now "over-dipped" the receipts by $12.90.

The next morning, D. McCarthy was told that unless he repaid the $12.90 at once, he would not be allowed to continue to work for the company. Although, as he testified, he was ready to repay the $12.90, D. McCarthy was determined not to be intimidated. He took his bus out as usual without returning the money. He was stopped shortly thereafter by his supervisor, J.J. McCarthy and the two McCarthys rode back to the garage in silence.

The dispute would not have ended if a strike had not begun the next day. The strike lasted 29 days, at which time D. McCarthy not only repaid the $12.90 but indicated that he was also ready to agree on a temporary truce and to accept reinstatement as the union requested. But he persisted in seeking arbitration to remove the cloud the company had placed over his honesty and integrity. To present his case in a hearing before me, D. McCarthy was required to take a day off from work.

The issues I was asked to decide were (1) whether D. McCarthy should be reimbursed for the day's work he lost and (2) whether he should be paid for the day he lost to argue for the day's pay he lost. I issued the following Conclusions of Fact:

"1. D. McCarthy is a man of honor.
2. D. McCarthy cannot be intimidated.
3. D. McCarthy is a stubborn man.
4. These attributes are not possessed exclusively by D. McCarthy, but belong as well to J.J., J.T. and J.E. McCarthy.
5. This dispute has now run its natural course. It must be brought to a swift conclusion."

On the basis of the foregoing findings of fact, I issued the following award:

"1. D. McCarthy is directed to cease and desist from 'dipping' into the company's receipts.
2. The Company is directed to cease and desist from 'dipping' into McCarthy's pay check.
3. The Company is directed to restore D. McCarthy's record to

the same spotless condition it was in before this unfortunate affair began.

4. D. McCarthy is directed to continue to render the Company the same honest and efficient service he has for the last 18 years.

5. Since it would be unfair to award D. McCarthy reimbursement for both the day he lost through suspension and the day he lost to recover the day he lost, and unkind to deny him reimbursement for both days, he is hereby awarded one full day's pay."

TEN COMMANDMENTS FOR ARBITRATORS

I. Decide the dispute strictly in accordance with the mandate the parties have given you; do not substitute your judgment of fairness for the criteria you are called upon to apply. Simply splitting the difference is a cop-out.

II. If the dispute involves the rights of the parties under a contract, guide yourself by the contract's terms, which usually limit you to an interpretation and application of the contract. You have no authority to add to, subtract from or modify its terms.

III. If interest claims are involved, guide yourself by the criteria in the stipulation of the parties submitting the dispute to arbitration.

IV. Conduct yourself as a judge would, without the black robes or elevated presence.

V. Avoid speaking to one party in the absence of the other, even on matters unrelated to the arbitration; it is extremely bad form if the matter has to do with the arbitration.

VI. Try to mediate if the opportunity arises. But neither say, nor do, anything in mediation that might prejudice your ability to make a decision on the merits.

VII. Confine your decision and opinion to the case before you. Omit any incidental or supplementary remarks. (The lawyers call it *obiter dicta*.)

VIII. Do not allow anyone unconnected with the arbitration to be present at the hearing without the consent of both sides.

IX. Do not release your decision to the public without the consent of both sides.

X. Agree in advance on how you will be paid.

CHAPTER SEVEN

TOO MANY COOKS

Boards of Mediators and Arbitrators

MEDIATION is a highly personal undertaking. Results depend heavily on the way people react to one and other. It is better undertaken by one person rather than a board of mediators. But there are distinct advantages in having a board of mediators in certain disputes. The mere presence on a panel of a person widely respected by the disputants may be reassuring to both sides.

At times a panel of mediators or arbitrators is selected, usually to include members whose presence might be reassuring to both sides. I prefer to act alone as a mediator in interest disputes, and as an arbitrator in rights disputes. I favor tripartite boards of arbitration in interest disputes with each side naming one arbitrator and the two selecting a third or neutral arbitrator.

Edward C. Maguire, who served as labor advisor to New York's Mayor William O'Dwyer, was a pioneer in the use of citizen mediators. I was his deputy for a time and then took his place when he resigned to return to private practice. Together we were involved in the selection of some unusual combinations of mediators who were effective either because they were very familiar with the disputants or because they enjoyed their respect.

In one dispute between the managers and the grooms and stable boys at the race tracks in New York City, we selected a panel consisting of Arthur Daley of the *New York Times* and Dan Parker of the *New York Daily Mirror,* two leading sports columnists, and Arthur Sloan of the State Racing Commission.

On another occasion, we asked New York Senator Herbert Lehman to mediate a dispute involving New York's manufacturers of ladies garments and the members of the International Ladies Garment

Workers Union (ILGWU). Both sides embraced his selection and strove diligently to reach an agreement to avoid embarrassing him.

But David Dubinsky, the shrewd president of the ILGWU during its years of greatest influence, was reluctant to mediate a dispute between two unions, both of whom had asked me to persuade Dubinsky to mediate their differences. He replied to my inquiry by asking rhetorically: "If it can be settled, why do they need me? If it can't be settled, why should I become involved."

Negotiation Between and Among Members of Panels of Neutrals

There are, obviously, cases in which the members of a board or panel of mediators or arbitrators disagree with each other. As a general rule, such disagreements are not as critical in an arbitration as they might be in a mediation. If arbitrators disagree, the decision of the majority determines the outcome. Since the arbitrators often negotiate with each other, it is essential, to ensure there will be a majority vote, that the board or panel be composed of an odd number of arbitrators. In that way there will always be a majority vote regardless of the differences among the arbitrators.

I took part in a major waterfront dispute in which I disagreed on a key issue with my two fellow mediators on a board of mediation that was required to make recommendations. I faced the question of how, if at all, I should express my disagreement with them. Our mission was to resolve the dispute. The decision of my fellow members would be projected as the recommendations of the board. It would hardly further the cause of agreement if I wrote a dissenting opinion. As a compromise, I simply included a single sentence in the board's report indicating that I preferred an approach to the key issue based on an annual guarantee of 1,600 hours.

This one sentence ultimately led to a solution that completely reformed longshoring on New York's waterfront. The basic facts and issues are worth recounting.

The Dock Strikes that Revolutionized the Waterfront

During the late 1950s and early 1960s, the relations of the International Longshoremen's Association (ILA) and the New York Shipping Association (Association) were in constant turmoil. Strikes regularly followed the expiration of successive two-year collective bargaining agreements.

On four occasions after the comprehensive labor bill known as the Taft-Hartley Act was adopted in 1947, the President of the United States invoked the statutory 80-day cooling-off period to prevent a waterfront strike. After the cooling-off period that expired on December 23, 1962, the New York area locals of the ILA struck, and the result was a tie-up of shipping in ports along the entire Atlantic and Gulf Coasts from Maine to Texas. Some 550 ships and more than 100,000 longshore and maritime workers were idled, and the nation's economic losses were estimated to be in the millions of dollars per day.

President Kennedy, brandishing a threat of compulsory arbitration legislation by Congress and citing the possibility of an economic disaster in the U.S. and throughout the world, along with delays in the delivery of foreign aid, relief and military equipment, announced the appointment of a mediation board. It was headed by Senator Wayne Morse, with Professor James Healy of the Harvard Business School and myself as members.

Before I was appointed to the board, Secretary of Labor Willard Wirtz asked me whether I would be prepared to recommend compulsory arbitration if that became the only possible solution. I said that if there was absolutely no other alternative, I would make such a recommendation.

The President gave us five days to achieve a settlement or recommend that Congress impose arbitration, a drastic measure. The key issue was the size of the dock gangs that loaded and unloaded ships. The employers were insisting on reductions in gang size, which they viewed as unnecessarily large in light of improved methods of loading and unloading ships. There were also complaints about featherbedding and other inefficient and corrupt practices related to the so-called shape-up method of selecting the members of the gangs.

During negotiations before the Morse panel was convened, the parties had agreed to a fact-finding study by the Department of Labor covering gang size, work force flexibility, severance pay, register closing, automation and other related problems. The study was to be completed by July 31, 1964.

The matters to be addressed in the special study centered around the shape-up which, it was charged, invited corruption, inefficiency, and inequality in wages and work opportunities.

At the daily shape-up on each pier, hiring bosses selected the workers from those who appeared, sometimes including their favorites—who might be a source of kickbacks if they did any work at all. Checks could be made payable to dead persons or those no longer working on the docks, and the proceeds pocketed by the hiring boss or his cronies. Even without a corrupt hiring boss or *mob* involvement, the system was inefficient because the departure of vessels could be delayed if an insufficient number of longshoremen showed up to load or unload them.

Many of those who shaped up were casual workers, even including lawyers, doctors or other professional men who came occasionally to work a day or two on the docks. Separate local unions controlled different piers with jurisdictional jealousies and each local gave preferential treatment to its own members; a longshoreman from Brooklyn could not work at Port Newark, for example, and if a junior member of one local declined a job, senior members from other locals could not be hired.

Members seeking work shaped-up at designated piers. If a ship did not arrive at their pier, they could be sent to piers where there was work. In the meantime the gangs at those piers could not start work until the requisite 21 members of the gang had been selected. Countless hours of work were lost by the time it took for workers to travel to the pier with work.

Costly shortages of labor in the busier sections of the port and excesses of labor elsewhere occurred due to the rush of cargo-ship masters who wanted to be put out to sea on Thursdays and Fridays to avoid time-and-a-half payments for labor on weekends. Excess labor could have been reduced by closing the registers of the bi-state Waterfront Commission, which had issued 27,000 licenses to dock workers and maintained hiring halls throughout the Port.

With the existing agreements due to expire on September 30, 1964, Secretary of Labor Wirtz reconvened the board that had settled the 1963 strike, clothing it with authority to make non-binding recommendations if necessary. Senator Morse resigned from the panel shortly thereafter, pleading the pressure of his Senate duties, and Assistant Secretary of Labor James Reynolds was designated chairman in his place.

The critical issues remained the Association's demand that the work gang be reduced in size from 20 to 15 and the ILA's insistence on guarantees for the employees who would lose work as a result. The panel was in accord on the reduction in gang size. But Reynolds and Healy proposed a formula on guarantees with which I disagreed. It was based on the number of hours a longshoreman had worked the previous year, which would, in my opinion, unfairly penalize longshoremen who, for illness, personal choice or other circumstances, worked only part time during the previous year.

During the years I have been involved in the affairs of labor and management, I have found that disparate treatment, whether between employees or competing employers, can cause more dissension than any other single factor. I based my belief that the formula wouldn't work on the operations of the "me-too" syndrome, common in labor-management relations and indeed in all human relations—everyone wants to be fed from the same spoon.

As an alternative, I proposed that regular employees be guaranteed 16 hundred hours or 40 weeks of work a year. My alternative evolved out of discussions during the negotiations of the union's proposal that there be a guaranteed annual wage. The proposal was strongly opposed by the Employers as prohibitively costly. I reasoned that with holidays, vacations and unemployment compensation, the Employers could afford the guarantee I was proposing.

While I differed from my colleagues on the formula for calculating the guaranteed annual wage, I did not file a formal dissent since I did not want my minority views to stand in the way of a settlement. Instead I simply proposed and my colleagues agreed, that I be allowed to insert a single sentence in the body of the text proposing a guarantee of sixteen hundred hours a year for all regular employees. I made no arguments for or against either my formula or the formula my colleagues proposed.

Negotiations on the new contract collapsed on September 30 when the ILA rejected the board's proposal. The longshoremen struck, closing ports from Maine to Texas. The Johnson Administration immediately secured a Taft-Hartley injunction, with the 80 days expiring December 20, 1964. At that point, absent a settlement, the strike could resume. Once the injunction was granted, the board resumed efforts for a settlement.

Four days before the December 20 deadline, the ILA and the Employers reached agreement on a four-year contract based on the one-sentence recommendation I had made. It prevented a renewal of the strike and revolutionized the way ships were loaded and unloaded in the past.

The guarantee solved other problems of the waterfront. With the guarantee (increased by agreement in subsequent collective bargaining negotiations to a guaranteed annual wage), the longshoremen were required to show up for work or lose the guarantee. Under the previous shape up system, 50 thousand people were on the hiring lists, many with other jobs. With the guarantee, the work force was reduced to fifteen thousand regularly employed workers.

Besides, the guarantee enabled the Employers to assign work a day before a ship was to arrive. As a result, there is no waiting now for longshoremen to shape-up for work or to move from one pier to another, from Brooklyn to Newark, for example, after a ship arrives. The guarantee has also eliminated the deadbeats on the payroll, and the pier boss is no longer able to discriminate between and among work applicants or to demand favors and kickbacks.

The 1967 Railroad Strike: Negotiation Within the Arbitration Board

Negotiation among panel members also arose in a 1967 railroad labor dispute in which I served on a five-member arbitration board created by an Act of Congress. President Johnson was authorized by the legislation to name the members of the board. In addition to me, he selected Senator Morse of Oregon, AFL-CIO president George Meany, former Senator Leverett Saltonstall of Massachusetts, and Frederick Kappel, a former chairman of AT&T.

I learned of my appointment when I was awakened in a Paris hotel at 4 AM (as I was sleeping heavily after a dinner at a three-star restaurant), by a telephone call from President Johnson. He asked me if I could return immediately to serve on the arbitration board established by Congress. I left later that morning.

Congress had enacted the legislation after 137 thousand members of six shop craft unions—engineers, sheet metal workers, machinists, electricians and other skilled workers—struck the railroads.

The dispute was a classic example of "me-tooism." In their most recent agreement, the Brotherhood of Railroad Trainmen had obtained wage increases of 5% a year for each of two years. The shop crafts believed they were entitled to more. The railroads insisted on the same agreement for all railroad unions. If the shop crafts received more, the trainmen would surely be back for still more.

Employers dealing with more than one union and unions dealing with two or more companies must always reckon with "me-tooism." Not surprisingly, the shop craft unions, led by the International

Association of Machinists under President Roy Siemiller, were determined to break the pattern.

Our five-member board was not the first to grapple with the complexities of the issue in this dispute. An earlier effort by an emergency board had recommended that the pattern be preserved, but the unions rejected the recommendation.

Professor John Dunlop of Harvard University (later to serve as Secretary of Labor) was then appointed to mediate the dispute. After hearing the claims of both sides, he recommended an increase of 6% for 18 months. Dunlop's strategy was shrewd. His proposal would give the shop crafts more for the first twelve months than the trainmen would receive but they would get less for the next six months and then have to negotiate for the remaining six months of the trainmen's two-year contract. Both sides rejected Professor Dunlop's proposal—the railroads because it was a departure from the established pattern and the shop crafts because they were determined to get more for a two-year contract than the trainmen had negotiated.

The legislation Congress passed after Dunlop's proposal was rejected required the parties to show cause before our board why the 6% for 18 months should not be approved. Congress also said that there should be a 24-month contract, as the trainmen had negotiated. This meant that the board of arbitrators also had to decide what wage increase, if any, should be granted for the six months following the expiration of the 18 months.

We held hearings and took testimony, and the focus then shifted from the negotiations of the parties to negotiations between and among the arbitrators. A majority of three could make the award but unanimity was obviously preferable. As the only active participant in collective bargaining on the board, it became my lot to speak first on the solution I thought would be appropriate.

I opened by saying that I had heard no reason why the 6% for 18 months should be altered or any persuasive argument in favor of going beyond the total increase of 5% a year for each of two years. Senator Saltonstall and Fred Kappel nodded in approval. George Meany and Wayne Morse waited to hear what I would propose for the remaining six months.

I continued by saying that, for our award to be equivalent with the dollars the trainmen would receive under their agreement, we would have to award another 6% for the remaining six months, or a total award of 6% for 18 months and an additional 6% for six months.

Senator Saltonstall appeared puzzled. "You said that the pattern of 5-and-5 for 2 years should be maintained," he said. "If so shouldn't the award be 6% for 18 months and 4% for 6 months?"

My answer was that six for eighteen months and six for six months would give the employees the same number of dollars *during* the 2 years of the agreement as the trainmen would receive under their agreement of 5-and-5 for 2 years.

I have italicized the word "during" to emphasize that the comparison of equivalence I had given our board members applied solely to the actual dollars that would be paid during the two years, not the rate that would exist at the end of the two years.

While the total amount the shop crafts would receive would be the same as the trainmen, I continued, the 6-and-6 would give them a higher base from which to negotiate their next agreement. That is a significant advantage since it is easier to defend the status quo than to propose or oppose a change. For that reason, I said, I would recommend that 6% for 18 months be followed with 5% for the remaining 6 months.

I am not sure that I ever convinced Senator Saltonstall of my mathematics; certainly an editorial writer for the *New York Times,* after two telephone conversations with me, was not persuaded that we had not violated the voluntary wage stabilization rules the President was promoting. In any event, the board unanimously accepted my suggestion, the railroads and the shop crafts appeared satisfied, and that was the end of the dispute.

CHAPTER EIGHT

LEGAL RESTRAINTS AND THE VOLUNTARY TECHNIQUES

The Labor Law's Promotion of the Voluntary Techniques

THE National Labor Relations Act of 1935 as amended in 1947 governs the way labor and management in the private sector must deal with each other. As written in 1935, the law required employers to bargain with unions selected by a majority of their employees. As amended, the law placed a similar obligation on unions.

The law now defines collective bargaining as "the mutual obligation of the employer and the representative of the employees to meet at reasonable times and confer in good faith with respect to wages, hours and other terms and conditions of employment."

The law also states that collective bargaining includes "the negotiation of an agreement or any question arising thereunder, and the execution of a written agreement incorporating any agreement reached."

In these respects, the law equates collective bargaining with negotiation. It also grants both sides the indispensable negotiating right to disagree with each other. The duty to bargain collectively, the law makes clear, "does not compel either party to agree to a proposal or require the making of a concession."

In addition, the law entitles both sides to enforce their right to disagree by taking unilateral action in the event of an impasse in negotiations. For unions, it is the right to strike, which the law endorses by providing that the "quitting of labor" by an employee or employees shall not be construed an illegal act.

As confirmed by the courts, the law gives employers the reciprocal right to disagree by locking out their employees, or unilaterally imposing the terms and conditions they have been seeking provided they have bargained to an impasse in good faith. The latter option is by far the most practical for most employers.

The effectiveness of the right to disagree, as I have noted, depends on the power of the disputants to exercise the right, and *that* turns on their respective bargaining strength and skills as well as relevant economic, social and political circumstances. In times of high unemployment, the employer usually has the upper hand. If workers are in short supply, the union may be ahead. Obviously, there are other variables that can affect the outcome.

The intent of the law, as amended in 1947, was to create a level playing field on which bargaining or negotiating would be conducted, with the National Labor Relations Board (NLRB) as the umpire on the obligations of both sides to bargain in good faith. At times, one side or the other has greater bargaining strength. In the early days, the advantage in many cases was on the unions' side. At present, employers are ahead in most situations.

On occasion, one side or the other has complained about the way the law has been administered by the NLRB. They have also lobbied Congress about changing sections of the law. In recent years, labor has been particularly unhappy about the current application of a 1938 Supreme Court decision, which held that the law entitled employers to hire permanent replacements in an economic strike. The decision has come into active use following the replacement of almost all of the 15,000 air traffic controllers who struck at the outset of the Reagan administration. As I pointed out in Chapter One, Reagan was mandated to replace the controllers by a federal law that prohibits the employment of any federal employee who takes part in a strike. There is no such law in the private sector.

The Supreme Court has also ruled that, despite the provisions of the Norris-La Guardia Act, which bars injunctions in labor disputes, the courts can enjoin strikes or lockouts in disputes in which collective bargaining agreements provide for the arbitration of grievances. The courts will infer that the agreement prohibits strikes or lockouts if it contains a provision for the arbitration of grievances even in the absence of a specific no strike, no lockout pledge.

In sum, the system of labor/management relations in force in the United States at present contains a comprehensive framework guiding the way companies and unions are called upon to conduct themselves. It covers all aspects of their relation from the beginning of union organization to the conclusion and renewal of collective bargaining agreements, as well as their review and enforcement through mediation, arbitration and administrative board or court actions.

The provisions of the law cover the full range of techniques of conflict prevention and resolution tried and tested over the years by companies, unions, the NLRB and the Courts. It has led me to conclude that this comprehensive and recorded body of experience can serve effectively as a useful model for comparison and analysis of the techniques of conflict prevention and resolution in other group relationships. This conclusion, as well as my involvement in many labor-management disputes, accounts for the frequent references in this book to the experience of labor and management in bargaining collectively with each other.

With the passage of time, readjustments in dynamic relationships are unavoidable. The negotiation and renegotiation of collective bargaining agreements provide companies and unions with the opportunity periodically to make creative adjustments in their relationships. The negotiations traditionally begin with adversarial challenges and almost invariably end in agreements with no-strike, no lockout provisions that assure both sides stability in their relationship for the term of the collective bargaining agreements. These renegotiations can also produce novel solutions to difficult problems.

The law provides for mediation in the event of an impasse in negotiations over the terms of collective bargaining agreements. As I have previously noted, negotiators at impasse are generally reluctant to propose mediation out of fear their opponent will consider the proposal a sign of weakness. The law solves that problem by requiring the Federal Mediation and Conciliation Service and relevant state mediation agencies to be notified 60 days before onset or expiration of collective bargaining agreements and to appear on the scene 30 days before the due date.

With the endorsement of the Supreme Court in the three notable decisions known as the Steelworkers Trilogy, the law has encouraged the arbitration of grievances arising during the term of collective bargaining agreements as the law of the workplace. The law also permits the parties to engage in the voluntary arbitration of interest disputes if they so desire.

Since the law was amended in 1947, the NLRB has ruled in thousands of cases on various aspects of negotiation, mediation and arbitration. The courts have also made relevant rulings in reviewing the NLRB's decisions and companies and unions have guided themselves in accordance with the rulings. In my opinion, this body of experience can be used for illustrative comparisons of the ways in which the voluntary techniques of conflict resolution are used in specific situations. Beyond the fact that the National Labor Relations Act requires employers and unions to negotiate with each other in good faith, the law is otherwise an affirmation of the voluntary techniques of conflict resolution.

The following section of this Chapter and the next Chapters describe three exceptional situations in which legal restraints have affected the way in which labor and management deal with each other. They also throw light on the uses of the voluntary techniques of conflict resolution.

Legal Restraints on the Right of Public Employees to Strike

Strikes in the public sector, unlike the private sector, are generally prohibited by law or judicial determination in virtually all jurisdictions in the United States. In turn, the right of the employing governmental agency to lockout or unilaterally impose employment changes after good faith bargaining is also limited. The experiences of labor and government in the public sector in light of these restrictions on their right to disagree can help sharpen our understanding of the techniques of conflict resolution.

Without an unqualified right to disagree, management and labor in the public sector have devised alternative strategies. They are sufficient to qualify mutual discussions in the public sector as negotiation. What is still under debate is whether these discussions constitute collective bargaining as that term is used in private sector labor-management negotiations.

A strike is the principal way in which employees in the private sector can exercise their right to disagree when an employer rejects demands for changes in the status quo.

The right of an employer unilaterally to impose the changes in the status quo he is seeking is the principal way in which an employer exercises his right to disagree. It is these rights, of employees to strike and employers to act unilaterally after good faith bargaining, that currently underpin the private sector's process of negotiation called collective bargaining.

The Impact on Bargaining of the Ban on Strikes by Public Employees

In the public sector, the right of public employees to strike against their employer, the government, had been challenged as illegal under common law. It had not been prohibited by statute before public employees became interested in the right to organize and bargain collectively after private sector employees were guaranteed such rights in the 1947 Labor/Management Relations Act (Taft-Hartley). That enactment, which made substantial amendments to the 1935 National Labor Relations Act (also known as the Wagner Act), rounded out the model of negotiation we are using for comparison with other established group relationships.

In most jurisdictions in the United States today—i.e., in the federal, state and city services of most of our governmental entities—the right to strike is now prohibited by specific statutory enactment.

Although there had been employee organizations in the public sector, they tended to call themselves associations instead of unions, and they generally frowned upon strikes. Nor did they engage in collective bargaining, as the term is understood in the private sector. The wages and working conditions of civil servants were set by legislative enactment, not through negotiations with union representatives. For the most part, the associations relied on lobbying to enforce their demands. They would also meet and confer with public employers on employment matters, but they rarely asserted the right to bargain collectively with its implicit inclusion of the right to strike.

In 1868, Congress adopted the eight-hour day for all government employees. It enacted the Civil Service Act in 1883, which remains the primary statute governing the method of appointment to the federal service. New York adopted a civil service or merit system of employment in the same year. It was the first state to adopt such a system. The New York City Employees' Retirement System, a pioneering approach to civil service, was established on October 1, 1920. Section 220 of the Labor Laws of New York, enacted in 1921, granted public employees the rates of pay prevailing in comparable classifications in the private sector.

The first New York State statutory prohibition against strikes by public employees was adopted in 1947 in the wake of a strike by teachers in Buffalo, New York. The legislation proposed at that time by then-Governor Thomas E. Dewey became the Condon-Wadlin Law, which specifically prohibited strikes by public employees. It also imposed a penalty of the loss of two days pay for every day a public employee participated in a strike.

In a statement he made when he signed the law, Governor Dewey enunciated what was the general rule with regard to public employee-employer relationships up to that time. He justified the prohibition of strikes by saying that public employees had the right to petition their employer for the correction of wrongs in the employment relationship, the right to electioneer and to elect into office their employers and the right to lobby the legislature to enact legislation in their favor. In addition, public employees had the right to select a spokesman to represent them when they petitioned their employer for the redress of grievances, a right all citizens enjoy under our Constitution. He emphasized, however, that the decision of the public employer was final. The only alternative for the employees was to lobby to overturn the decision.

These basic procedures of employee organizations were challenged by the Transport Workers Union (TWU) beginning in 1939, when city government took over New York City's two privately owned subway systems—the IRT and the BMT—and unified them with the IND, which the City had built and was operating. The three lines were placed under the control of the Board of Transportation (later renamed the Transit Authority).

Prior to unification, the employees of the IRT and BMT were represented by the Transport Workers Union (TWU) and had collective bargaining agreements with those lines similar to union agreements in the private sector. They included recognition of the TWU as the exclusive bargaining representative of the employees.

Ironically, it was Fiorello H. LaGuardia, a mayor known widely as a friend of labor, who affirmed the position of the Board of Transportation that, as civil servants, the city's transit workers were not entitled to the collective bargaining rights they enjoyed as private sector employees. In particular, the Board of Transportation ruled as illegal the right of private sector unions representing a majority of the employees to exclusive recognition. That opened the door to the organization of transit workers by rival unions in various units. The Board of Transportation also opposed as illegal the TWU's demands for a written collective bargaining agreement, the union shop, a checkoff and the arbitration of grievances.

The TWU voiced strenuous objections at the time. But in 1941 the country became involved in World War II, and with the war in progress, the issue of the right of public workers to bargain collectively was not faced until 1945. In the absence of private sector bargaining rights and the protection of a collective bargaining agreement, the TWU's membership dwindled dramatically during the war years.

Faced with the prospect of even greater losses, Mike Quill, TWU's fiery president, took a bold gamble: he threatened the first citywide transit strike in the history of public employee labor relations and made exclusive recognition of all transit workers the union's principal demand. Mayor William O'Dwyer responded to Quill's threatened strike by appointing a panel headed by General David Sarnoff, then chairman of RCA. There followed the first of many all-night sessions at City Hall, out of which came an agreement to submit the disputed issues to a five member fact-finding panel headed by Arthur S. Meyer, the chairman of the New York State Board of Mediation. I was one of the five members. We held hearings and issued a report that was hailed as a milestone in public sector bargaining relationships. In retrospect, it looks rather mild.

Acting on the legal advice of the City's corporation counsel, we recommended against exclusive bargaining rights but proposed that the TWU be the first among equals since it was the largest union on the property. We also ruled against a written contract, but we added that any terms agreed upon should be incorporated in a memorandum of understanding to facilitate future reference. We voted against the arbitration of grievances, the union shop and the deduction of dues from employee's paycheck (known as a check-off), but we proposed advisory or non-binding arbitration as a legal alternative.

Changes in subsequent years brought the relationship of the TWU with the Transit Authority (which replaced the Board of Transportation in 1951) closer to the collective bargaining model in the private sector. Despite Condon-Wadlin's ban on strikes by public workers, the TWU continued to rely on the ploy John L. Lewis had popularized: "no contract, no work," a threat Quill made to sound sufficiently credible for the Transit Authority to take as real.

In the meantime, the experience of the Transport Workers Union proved to be contagious. The benefits the TWU was achieving were attractive to other public employee organizations. Soon the teachers, then the sanitation workers and firemen, began to talk about collective bargaining; in due course, the police officers, who had their own Patrolmen's Benevolent Association, followed suit. Most of these organizations used the word "association" to indicate a distinction between their type of organization and a private sector union. In the beginning, these organizations did not claim the right to strike or the right to bargain collectively. But as they saw other public sector organizations opting for collective bargaining and winning significant wage and benefit improvements, they also began clamoring for that right without giving up their rights to meet and confer, to lobby, to electioneer or to utilize Section 220 of the Labor Law on prevailing rates of pay.

Mayor Wagner's 1958 Executive Order— The "Little Wagner Act"

In 1954, Robert F. Wagner, Jr. became Mayor of New York City. In 1958, he promulgated an executive order modeled after the National Labor Relations Act that his father had sponsored; this was heralded as the "little Wagner Act" for public employees. It spoke of their right to organize and their right to bargain collectively without addressing the question of their right to strike.

There followed a substantial degree of union organization with the main issue being recognition. The units for recognition were rather haphazardly selected. As a result, at one point the city had to deal with the representatives of about 150 employee groups. There has been a trend toward consolidation of the various groups and there are now six dominant labor organizations of New York City employees: police, fire, sanitation, teachers, transport workers and District Council 37 of the State, County and Municipal Employees, a latecomer catch-all for groups otherwise unorganized. It has become the largest labor organization in New York City.

The era of organization which occurred during the Wagner years had reached the point of collective bargaining by 1966, when John V. Lindsay succeeded Mayor Wagner. Primarily as the result of the tacit or sometimes explicit threats to strike that the increasingly aggressive public sector labor organizations utilized, their relations with the city moved more and more in the direction of the collective bargaining relations of private sector bargaining. But the ambivalence continued over the right of public employees to strike.

On New Year's Eve, December 31, 1965, hours after he had been sworn in, John Lindsay faced the threat of a citywide bus and subway strike over the wage demands of the TWU.

In a last ditch effort to prevent a strike, Mayor Lindsay proposed arbitration. On behalf of the TWU, Quill dismissed the proposal and the strike began at 5AM on January 1, 1966. Quill was jailed for contempt of an injunction barring the strike. While in jail, he suffered a heart attack and was put in an oxygen tent in Bellevue Hospital. On the eleventh day of the devastating strike, Mayor Lindsay asked the three member board of mediation (of which I was one) to recommend terms of settlement. But we, the mediators, had agreed in advance with both sides that we would not make recommendations.

I then suggested that we might advise the mayor of the terms we thought were appropriate, and he promptly asked us for our advice. On receipt of the terms, the Mayor immediately made them public. The recommendations called for a substantial percentage increase to bring the skilled employees into line with prevailing rates without denying the unskilled workers the same percentage increase. They were accepted by both sides and ended the strike. But not the controversy.

The settlement provoked a taxpayer lawsuit to cancel the wage increases as invalid under existing law and to impose a suspension of two days pay on the employees for each of the eleven days they were on strike. Judge Bernard Botein notified the Mayor that he had no choice but to set the agreement aside and to impose the fine. While this was going on, Quill died of a heart attack. His successor, Matthew Guinan, faced the unattractive alternatives of either accepting invalidation of the settlement and imposition of the fines or leading his members in another illegal strike.

Guinan recognized that another strike would be foolhardy but he was at a loss over how to cope with the severe penalties his members would suffer if he took no action. Guinan appealed for help to Harry Van Arsdale, the dynamic and creative head of New York City's Central Labor Council of unions affiliated with the American Federation of Labor/Congress of Industrial Organizations. Van Arsdale turned to Governor Nelson A. Rockefeller for assistance.

The governor immediately grasped the depths of the dilemma that Guinan and the labor movement faced. But he also had to address the underlying question of the right of public workers to bargain effectively with their public employer without relying on the right to strike. The Condon-Wadlin Law had dismissed this question as inapplicable in the public sector.

Governor Rockefeller took two bold steps: 1) he introduced legislation that was passed immediately repealing the penalty provisions of Condon-Wadlin as applied to the transit workers alone, and 2) he named a five-member committee of experts headed by the distinguished dean of labor/management relations, Professor George W. Taylor of the University of Pennsylvania, to write a new law governing public sector employment relations.

The committee's report was adopted in 1967 and, with some amendments, has been the statutory basis governing the relations of New York State's public employees and their employers since that time. It has also been adopted with modifications in other states.

Our experience with the law reveals its strengths and weaknesses. It also underscores the differences between collective bargaining in the private and public sectors. The Taylor Committee agreed that public employees should not have the right to strike. But it disagreed with the concept implicit in Condon-Wadlin that public workers should not have the right to participate through unions of their choosing in the decision-making of their employment terms and conditions.

Collective Negotiation: A New Concept in a New Law

Recognizing that in the absence of the right to strike, there could not be collective bargaining as it is practiced in the private sector, the committee chose to use the words "collective negotiation" as a right public employees could choose to exercise, but never defined the term. Nor was the term defined in the new law, appropriately called the Taylor Law, which the legislature adopted on the basis of the report of the Taylor Committee.

In practice, as well as in the rest of the law, the term "collective negotiation" was used as if it possessed the same meaning as collective bargaining. Indeed, in a Court of Appeals decision upholding compulsory arbitration of police and fire disputes, Judge Jasen spoke of disputes arising "in the course of collective bargaining negotiations."

To grant public workers bargaining rights comparable to those that employees in the private sector possessed, the Taylor law followed the structure and form of the National Labor Relations Act. Like the NLRA, it granted public employees the right of organization and representation and set up procedures for determining representation. It also imposed on "the state, local governments and other subdivisions" the duty "to negotiate with, and enter into written agreements with employee organizations" which had been duly certified or recognized. In addition, it designated as an "improper" practice for a public employer "to refuse to negotiate in good faith" with the duly recognized or certified representative of its employees. And it created a Public Employment Relations Board (PERB) to administer the law as the NLRB administers the NLRA.

The Taylor law expressly continued the prohibition against strikes by public workers. Two consequences necessarily flowed from this, neither present in the private sector. First, it became necessary (this was also true of Condon-Wadlin) to prescribe penalties for violations. Secondly, it was also necessary (and this was new in the Taylor law) to prescribe alternate procedures to the strike for resolution of disputes in the event of an impasse in bargaining.

The primary alternate procedure, in addition to mediation—which is not an alternate procedure but an aid to bargaining—is fact-finding with recommendations. But recommendations can, by definition, be rejected. In consequence, it was necessary to prescribe an alternative to fact-finding with recommendations in the event of rejection by either or both sides.

The Taylor Committee suggested that the legislative body with jurisdiction hold a form of "show cause hearing" at which the parties would review their positions with respect to the recommendations and the legislative body would then enact appropriate budgetary allotments or other regulations.

The statute as originally passed did not include this proposal, since the State Legislature was not keen on assuming the burden of finally deciding public employee disputes. This left public sector unions with no place to go if they accepted the recommendations and the public employer rejected them.

A 1969 amendment provided that, after the legislative body or a duly authorized committee held a hearing at which the parties explained their positions with respect to the report of the fact-finding board, "the legislative body shall take such action as it deems in the public interest, including the interest of the public employees involved." Very few public employee disputes have ever reached that level.

Unresolved Issues Under the Taylor Law

Also unresolved is what should be done if the legislative body and the public employer, the Transit Authority for example, are one and the same, and the Transit Authority is called upon as a legislator to pass on its offer as an employer.

Strictly construed, this procedure means that the final decision-maker remains the legislative body and, in most instances, the state legislature. This is, obviously, very different from joint decision-making by private unions and employers. It does accord with Governor Dewey's view that government must be the final decision-maker on employment matters. But it contains intervening procedures designed to bring about agreements that Condon-Wadlin omitted.

Despite the severity and variety of the penalties, the Taylor law has not stopped strikes by public workers. Nor is it likely to do so. It is difficult to penalize employees in the public sector for conduct approved in the private sector by workers performing the same or similar work and facing the same economic problems.

The Metropolitan Transportation Authority is an umbrella organization that includes the Transit Authority and the Long Island Rail Road. Both operate in and out of Penn Station but are subject to different rules on strikes. The Transit Authority's subway and bus employees are subject to the absolute strike prohibition of the Taylor Law. The employees of the Long Island Rail Road, which is subject to the Federal Railway Labor Act, can strike after the restraining procedures of that law have been exhausted.

It is also difficult to devise penalties that make sense. Who should be punished: the employees who strike or their leaders who advise them to strike? The Taylor Law deals with both and allows the Public Employee Relations Board (PERB) to determine how the penalties should be applied. The suspension of the dues check-off is generally viewed as punishment directed at the leadership. But if the union is bereft of funds, it becomes handicapped in servicing its members. Similarly, if its leaders are jailed for violations, the employees lose the benefits of their leadership.

But public sector employees are not without remedies. As noted, they can lobby their bosses, an advantage private sector employees do not enjoy. They can campaign for or against them, and their support or opposition can be meaningful, as politicians regularly recognize. They have also become adept in the politics of governmental affairs and they are not shy about using their skills. The result is that there are meaningful mutual discussions between public sector unions and the public bosses of their members.

Public Sector Negotiations and Government Affairs

Whether the term "collective bargaining" is an accurate description of the discussions is debatable. But public sector negotiations have reached a stage of development that has made them a significant factor in government affairs. Actually, public sector union membership has been growing all the while private sector growth has been declining.

There is another aspect of the ban on strikes by public sector employees and the alternative procedures that must be substituted in its place. The alternatives reduce the capacity of public employers to take unilateral action in support of changes they seek in employment terms and conditions.

Public employers have different incentives than do their counterparts in the private sector. The latter are motivated mostly by what is frequently referred to as the bottom line. The public employer has his eye focused sharply on the next election. This frequently affects the form and outcome of public sector negotiations.

Whether called collective bargaining or not, the system of negotiation that has been building since the middle 1940's in public employment as the result of the experience of private employees in the making of collective bargaining agreements is unquestionably here to stay; but it is greatly different from its counterpart in the private sector.

CHAPTER NINE

THE VOLUNTARY TECHNIQUES
AND THE ANTITRUST LAWS

The Turmoil in Professional Sports

A 234-DAY strike consumed most of the 1995 baseball season. In 1998, a lockout almost ended basketball's entire season. Football and hockey have also had their share of labor disruptions.

The troubles are surely not the product of any lack of diligence or intelligence on the part of the owners and players. They are very mindful of their rights and obligations under law and they have vigorously and persistently pursued and defended them through the highest courts in the land. If a foolish consistency is the hobgoblin of little minds, the owners and unions in professional sports must be geniuses.

Why, then, you might ask, are they so fiercely in conflict with each other? Yes, the financial stakes are high. But at the root of the conflict, in my opinion, is the two tier system of bargaining that has grown into its present form as the owners and players exercised their rights and respected their obligations under the laws governing labor-management relationships and combinations condemned as illegal restraints of trade under the antitrust laws.

Unions exist to bargain collectively in behalf of their members. As the representative of a majority of the employees in an appropriate bargaining unit, they have the *exclusive* right and *duty* under the National Labor Relations Act to bargain for all employees in the unit. But unlike virtually all other unions, the representatives of the players in professional sports determinedly waive their right to bargain collectively on all salaries except the minimum entrance rate. Instead, they empower their members to bargain *individually* on compensation, simply reserving for themselves the remaining terms and conditions of employment permitted by law.

I learned of the waiver in the 1960s when I was representing the

National Football League on labor matters. At the time, the National Football League Players Association was competing with the International Brotherhood of Teamsters for the right to represent the players in collective bargaining. The owners agreed with the Association to ascertain the wishes of the players by having David L. Cole, a noted arbitrator, conduct a check of cards authorizing the Association to represent them. To the relief of the owners, the Association emerged as the clear choice of the players. The owners were then ready, as required by law, to recognize the Association as the *exclusive* representative of the players on salaries, hours and working conditions, the subjects both sides must respect. But the Association insisted on waiving the right and duty to bargain on salaries and the owners readily accepted the waiver.

Unions in industry would commit mayhem before waiving their statutory right to bargain collectively on compensation. Conversely, employers would jump with joy if a union representing their employees gave up its right to bargain on compensation.

The Bargaining Strength of the Superstars

The genius of both sides can be found in the motivation for their untraditional role reversals. In professional sports, the superstars have far more leverage bargaining individually than they would have if the union bargained for them along with all other players. It is their unique skills that give them the bargaining strength to command millions in pay. Their bargaining strength would be significantly diluted if the union insisted on its exclusive statutory right to bargain collectively on salaries for all players

The Invalidation of the Reserve Systems' Restrictions

Before collective bargaining was introduced in professional sports, the owners had designed several formidable restrictions on player transfers from one club to another. Baseball was the pioneer in developing such restrictions. To begin with, the owners agreed among themselves to "reserve" 15 of the 25 eligible players on their roster: no other club could bid for the services of the 15 players.

The baseball owners also inserted a provision in the standard player contract that gave the owners the option, in the event of a disagreement over the terms of a new contract, to require the player to serve an additional year under the terms of the expiring contract plus ten percent. The net effect of the restrictions, which came to be known as the reserve system, was to reduce severely the bargaining leverage of the superstars.

With the arrival of collective bargaining, the unions challenged the restrictions and brought suits to have them declared illegal under the antitrust laws. The courts agreed and invalidated most of the restrictions. With no restraints on their ability to negotiate contracts with the club that would pay them the highest salary, the superstars quickly won salary increases that have now reached astronomical heights.

There was one notable exception to the invalidation of the reserve systems. A decision of the Supreme Court, written by the famed Justice Oliver Wendell Holmes, ruled in 1923 that baseball was a sport, not a trade, and was therefore exempt from the law's prohibitions against combinations in restraint of trade. As professional sports became more profitable, the Supreme Court ruled that boxing and other professional sports were trades within the meaning of the antitrust laws. In light of those rulings, the star baseball center fielder Curt Flood asked the Supreme Court to review baseball's exemption from the antitrust laws. The Supreme Court turned him down ruling that it was up to Congress to decide whether the exemption should be lifted since the parties had invested time and money in reliance on the Court's earlier ruling.

The Non-Statutory Labor Exemption from the Antitrust Laws

The decision turned out to be of little help to the baseball owners. An arbitrator, appointed pursuant to the collective bargaining agreement, ruled that as a matter of contract law the owner's option in the standard player contract was illegal. As a result, the baseball owners as well as the owners in all other professional sports now have to reckon with the bargaining strength of the superstars in negotiating with them on compensation. But another ruling has given them renewed collective bargaining leverage. It has become known as the non-statutory labor exemption from the antitrust laws.

To make collective bargaining meaningful, negotiators in multi-company bargaining must necessarily confer with each other in bargaining on wages, hours and working conditions, the so-called mandatory subjects of bargaining. But their joint deliberations and decisions could be construed as illegal combinations in restraint of trade. Since such a ruling would prevent an employer association from effectively engaging in collective bargaining, the Supreme Court concluded that the labor laws required the Court to exempt concerted action in collective bargaining from the restraints of the antitrust laws.

In effect, this ruling has opened the door to the negotiation of restrictions on the free movement of players from one team to another.

The unions, understandably, are dead set against such restrictions. They applaud the virtues of a free market while the owners continue to favor the imposition of restrictions through collective bargaining.

The 234-Day Baseball Strike of 1995

The baseball strike of 1995 grew out of a demand of the owners to bargain collectively on a salary cap for all players. The agreed upon amount would be allocated among the clubs pursuant to a formula the clubs would devise. No club would be permitted to pay more in compensation than the total limited by the cap. That would mean that if a superstar won a contract for many millions, there would be that much less for the other players.

The baseball union fought relentlessly against collective bargaining on all salaries. But the final settlement, after a series of legal maneuvers on both sides, included a collectively bargained tax on wages in excess of an agreed upon amount. The settlement did not satisfy the owners but it was a product of collective bargaining. Undoubtedly, the issue will be revisited in future negotiations with both sides keenly anxious to avoid another catastrophic strike.

The 1998 Basketball Lockout

A salary cap negotiated in collective bargaining was introduced years ago by the owners and players in basketball. But negotiated exceptions to the cap led the owners to seek modifications. The union was opposed to any change and the owners exercised their statutory right to lock the players out in the beginning of the 1998 season. The lockout was finally settled hours before a "crunch" date was about to come into force. See my discussion of the basketball crunch in Chapter Two.

The settlement of the lockout produced an innovation in the continuing conflict in professional sports over individual bargaining and collective bargaining. The new six-year collective bargaining agreement included the first limitation in professional sports on the salaries the superstars could receive. The caps are based on the players' years of service. No doubt the owners in other sports will be seeking similar restrictions on the salaries of their players.

In Chapter Two on the Burden of Going Forward, I described the strategic moves of labor and management in shifting the burden from one side to the other. Although the strike in baseball and the lockout in basketball involved substantially the same issue—collective versus individual bargaining—the response in baseball was taken by the union while in basketball the owners precipitated the shutdown by locking out the players. The difference is irrelevant to the underlying issue. It merely reveals the versatility of the owners and players in dealing with the complexities of bargaining in professional sports.

The Ultimate Solution: Resolution Through the Voluntary Techniques

The conflict over salaries in professional sports has now wound its way through the courts and has landed squarely on the bargaining table. There, both sides are called upon to devise mutually acceptable solutions using the voluntary techniques of conflict resolution. Since neither can exist without the other, they must find a solution they can both live with, and I am sure they will.

Composers and Lyricists: Employees or Independent Contractors?

From November 1971 and for 10 years thereafter, I represented the Composers and Lyricists Guild, whose members—including some of the best-known figures in American music—compose music and write lyrics for motion picture and television productions. I was retained by the Guild to negotiate with the Association of Motion Picture and Television Producers (AMPTP) representing the film companies on the issue of secondary "exploitation" (i.e., the use) of the music copyright. The existing collective bargaining agreement was to expire on November 30, 1971.

In motion pictures, the last creative contribution to the final product is made by the composer who is given the motion picture and a script indicating the number of seconds or minutes of music to compose to fit the mood of the picture: martial music if the film depicts a war, lyrical music if it is to accompany a romance, etc. By agreement of the parties and the rules of the American Society of Composers and Publishers (ASCAP), the music publisher and the composer each get fifty percent of the royalties. But the film producer controls the exploitation of the music.

The composers' complaint was that the producers allowed their music to accumulate on their shelves instead of seeking to exploit the music. In the simplest of terms, the composers were saying, "We wrote the music and you're not using it. We'd like to use it some other way."

Elmer Bernstein, president of the Guild, made the point in more formal terms. "Our greatest concern," he said, "is the fact that the greatest percentage of our music goes on the shelf, never to be seen or heard again."

Our negotiations with the AMPTP got nowhere and the Guild voted to strike at midnight November 30. The strike proved ineffective since the producers were able to send the film to Canadian and European composers.

Our next move was a suit under the antitrust laws, alleging that the producers were engaged in a conspiracy to restrain trade. We asked for $300 million in damages. The producers answered that they were exempt from the antitrust laws under the labor exemption, which allows unions and their members and employers in multi-employer negotiations to confer with each other on the terms of their negotiations. In the absence of the labor exemption, the conferring would be viewed as a conspiracy in violation of the antitrust laws.

We moved to strike their defense on the ground that the composers were independent contractors even though they had been certified as employees under the NLRB. Only employees and not independent contractors come under the jurisdiction of the National Labor Relations Act. An employee is defined as an employee who works under the direction and control of a supervisor. An independent contractor is on his own. We emphasized the point as I asked a talented composer where he did his best work. He said it was while driving in traffic. I then asked if there was anyone from management around telling him how to compose. The question drew a laugh and an inconclusive answer.

But the composer's testimony was not enough to convince Judge Charles Brieant, who threw our case out on the ground that it was hypocritical for the composers to claim they were independent contractors when they had sought and obtained NLRB certification as employees.

I argued the appeal before the Court of Appeals for the Second Circuit with Chief Judge Irving Kaufman presiding over the three-judge panel. My opponent was Simon Rose, an appellate lawyer from one of New York City's most prominent law firms. I opened by saying that Mr. Rose was a distinguished lawyer. I then added that Mr. Rose by any other name would still be a distinguished lawyer. "The composers called themselves employees," I said. "But they were in fact independent contractors."

It is not what they called themselves, I added, but what they are. When I saw Judge Kaufman nod his head, I knew we would win.

Three weeks after hearing the appeal, Judge Kaufman, speaking for a unanimous court, said that Judge Brieant "rang down the curtain on these talented artists but the curtain must rise again." The court remanded the case for further proceedings, which ultimately wound up in a satisfactory settlement.

WHAT'S AHEAD FOR ADR

As I have mentioned previously, every one of us is constantly engaged in negotiation in one form or another. That will continue to be true especially with the arrival of ADR. But we know now that our negotiating skills can be improved through training and practice.

Mediation will continue to grow rapidly in popularity, largely because there is little downside for either party. A mediator makes no decision and can rarely do any harm. Mediation is an art, not a science, and some come by the required capability instinctively. Others can enhance their talents through training and experience.

As disputants come to understand the advantages and limited liabilities of mediation, they are bound more and more to turn to mediation for conflict resolution. Former Senator George Mitchell's spectacular success as mediator in Ireland is a notable example. Richard Holbrooke has also done well in Bosnia and Kosovo.

The arbitration of rights disputes is also on the march. Many disputants are increasingly inclined to include as a term of on-going contracts a provision for the arbitration of future disputes arising during the life of the contract. Such a provision is already included in most labor/management collective bargaining agreements, as well as in many international agreements.

In negotiating a contract with such a provision, the parties generally limit the authority of the arbitrator to an interpretation and application of the terms of the agreement they have negotiated. This limitation on the authority of the arbitrator of rights disputes has been largely responsible for the growth of arbitration in on-going contractual relationships.

On the other hand, I do not see interest arbitration growing in the future. Disputants are reluctant to vest control of the resolution of interest disputes in the hands of a third party. They want to retain control for themselves. The parties can, of course, agree on the criteria an arbitrator must use in deciding an interest dispute. But if they can get that far, they usually can reach a settlement on their own.

In negotiating voluntarily with each other and in agreeing to mediation or arbitration, the disputants fashion their own form and forum of conflict resolution. The opportunities are vast for mutually satisfactory use of the voluntary techniques of conflict resolution.

The Trend Toward Conflict Management Systems

The law business has never been so good. Even as the cost of legal advice and assistance has been mounting, so also has the need for groups and individuals to turn to lawyers for help. But there has also been, as I mentioned earlier, a rising interest in conflict resolution encouraged to a large degree by the popularity of ADR. The voluntary cooling system of conflict resolution holds the greatest promise for reducing future conflicts as well as the cost and delays of litigation.

Toward that end, more and more companies and other organizations are moving to what is coming to be called "Conflict Management Systems." They include in one department the full range of voluntary techniques of conflict resolution—negotiation, mediation and arbitration—as well as their court and administrative law responsibilities. I hope that this book will help promote the trend.

INDEX

AAU. *See* Amateur Athletic Union
abortion issue, 5
academics, as arbitrators or mediators, 51, 88–89
Academy of Arbitrators, 51
Actors Equity, 89, 92
ADR. *See* Alternative Dispute Resolution
advisory arbitration, 9–10
affirmative action, 4–5
air traffic controllers, 29, 106
Allied Printing Trades Council, 34, 54
Alternative Dispute Resolution (ADR), xi–xii
   future of, 127–28
   techniques, 1, 9–12
Amateur Athletic Union (AAU), 87, 88
American Arbitration Association, 10, 50
American Federation of Musicians, 91
American Federation of State, County and Municipal Employees, 112
American Postal Workers Union, 86
Anaconda Copper and Wire, 9
Annan, Kofi, 30
antitrust laws, 119
   exemptions, 121–22, 124
Arafat, Yasser, 22
arbitration, xi–xii, 8
   accepting, 52
   advisory, 10
   announcing decision, 96
   in collective bargaining, 107
   compared to litigation, 53, 83, 88–89
   contracts requiring, 83, 90, 127
   enforceability, 87–88
   final offer selection, 11
   imposed by law, 86
   of interest disputes, 83, 84–86, 97, 127–28
   med-arb, 10
   rejection of, 84–86
   of rights disputes, 83–86, 90, 97, 126
   tripartite boards, 10–11, 87, 97, 98

arbitrators
   academics as, 51, 88–89
   compensation, 57
   focusing solely on issue, 91–92
   incentives, 49
   information on, 88
   lawyers as, 88
   negotiations among, 98, 102–4
   permanent, 90–91
   private meetings with each side, 56
   professional, 51
   role, 2
   selection of, 88–89
   skills, 51
   ten commandments for, 96
   use of judgment, 90–91
ARCO, 8–9
AT&T, 6
automobile industry, 17–18, 50

Bahr, Morton, 6
Ballow, Robert, 44, 45
bargaining table, 19–20
   See also negotiation
Barletta, Joseph F., 43
baseball, professional
   antitrust exemption, 121–22
   reserve system, 120–21
   strike (1995), 15, 53, 119, 122, 123
basketball, professional
   lockout (1998), 15, 16–17, 119, 122–23
   salary caps, 123
Benny, Jack, 28
Bernstein, Elmer, 124
bluffing, 36
boards
   arbitration, 10–11, 87, 97, 98
   mediation, 97, 99–102, 111, 113
Bosnia, 30, 126
Botein, Bernard, 113
Boulware, Lemuel, 38
Bradford, Amory H., 2–3
Brieant, Charles, 124